Bloom Where You Are

Bloom

Where You Are

CAROLYN HUFFMAN

VISION HOUSE PUBLISHERS
Santa Ana, California 92705

Library of Congress Catalogue Number 75-42853
ISBN-0-88449-024-6 (Paperback)

Printed in the United States of America.

To Carl
"And a little child shall lead them" (Isa. 11:6).

Acknowledgments

Because this is such a personal story, my own, I acknowledge in the book itself those special ones who have significantly influenced my life. There are so many others (especially my prayer groups) too numerous to mention who helped as I fell backwards, stumbled, walked along, or sometimes ran ahead in God's story.

I had no idea that preparing a book for publication was such a monumental task. I am deeply grateful to those who helped put it all together. Especially let me thank Carl and Honey Barlow (my father and mother), Keith and Mary Allen Miller, John and Lois Knox, Surrenden Angly, Dick and Eleanor Ann Chote, Leighton Ford, Marcia Foster, Danny and Mary Lou Henshaw, Ron and Ross Ogden, Dr. James Packer, Pat Pratt, Emma Ward, and Paul and Ernestlea Williams.

To my three girls, Beth, Heather, and Laura who kept insisting "Mama, you *can* write a book!" —

To my husband, Chuck, who insisted "Carolyn, you *must* write a book!" and then gave me the necessary encouragement and support to do so —

To all of you, God bless you for being there! I am so grateful that God put us in one another's bundle!

CAROLYN HUFFMAN

Contents

Foreword

I knew Carolyn Huffman was a communicator about seven years ago — the first time I heard her speak publicly. That night I saw a very frightened housewife stand before a large church filled with people. Since I knew she had never done anything like that before, I had no idea what to expect. I only knew that I had seen a quiet and remarkable kind of faith in the lives of Carolyn and her husband, Chuck, with whom we were becoming very close friends. Besides being an attractive couple, I knew they were very intelligent and that their adult lives had been drastically changed as a result of their trying to commit them to God.

As she waited, Carolyn was so frightened that I felt bad about having nudged her into speaking. But when she began, a strange thing happened: She was so frank and clear about her feelings that we were with her at once. Within a few minutes I realized that she wasn't *telling* us her story, she was *showing* it to us with word pictures. And she was doing it so unselfconsciously that she wasn't aware that she had captured us and was taking us by the hand up and down the halls of her memory, excitedly pointing here, or with a tear there, to some person or situation through which she had begun to grasp new meanings of life and death as a woman, wife, and mother.

When she finished speaking, she had succeeded in breaking a number of public-speaking rules, had taken 50 percent more time than had been allotted to her, and had ended her talk with a long poem *she had written*. Yet people weren't aware of any of these insurmountable errors. Something had happened to us while she was speaking, and things were different and better because she had shared her life.

A similar thing happened to me as I read this book. When I started, I thought maybe it was going to be like other books written by housewives who have become Christians. But before I knew it, I was caught up in the story and examining the tragedies, reflections, hopes, people, and circumstances Carolyn held up before me. When I had finished the last page, I realized that I had seen the Christian struggle with the problem of death, and particularly the loss of a child, more sensitively handled than I ever had before.

I wanted to buy a copy for every parent I knew who has lost a son or daughter. But the theme running through these pages is not death but rather life and change — vocational change, geographical change, and that most difficult change of all, a change in perspective about all of life.

Carolyn Huffman writes clearly and naturally and, in revealing her own story, somehow tells something of our stories as we face a world of change which seemingly ends with death. For people who have moved many times the "hardships" she describes may not seem severe, but the feelings of rootlessness will be very familiar.

I predict *Bloom Where You Are* will help thousands to find God in the midst of their agony and that it will bring a fresh breath of hope to Christians of all kinds — as it has for me today.

KEITH MILLER
Port Aransas, Texas

1

Turtles Live So Long

Birthdays are happy days — aren't they? Today then I should be having a party, blowing up balloons, setting out favors, baking a cake, and placing seven bright candles on that cake — seven, and one to grow on. But there was to be no party, no laughter, no presents, no balloons, no favors, no cake, no "Happy Birthday," no candles, for there was no Carl.

In the midst of my misery I sat and dared to put together — one by one — fierce, fragmented memories. Not very long ago, before the nightmare began, I had the world encased in a private terrarium, enjoying a smug, contented existence. I had a happy marriage with a loving husband, Chuck, an engineer who had vowed to make a million dollars by the time he was forty. I had a handsome six-year-old son, Carl, and a beautiful three-year-old daughter, Beth Ann. The future was all filed away under the heading: Rosy Hue — No Trespassing, Please. As to God, I vaguely believed in him as a remote creator but had no sense of his personal presence, much less of the fact that he had plans for me — a story for me to walk in. Had someone told me this, I doubt that I would have been interested. In the spring of 1959 I was much too involved walking in my own story to have any time left over for God's.

In 1956 my controlled, peaceful life had been frighteningly interrupted; briefly I sensed my inability to keep things the way I wanted them. Beth Ann was born a blue baby with a congenital heart defect. She had little chance for survival, and her condition worsened each hour she lived. When she was only two and one-half days old, Dr. Denton Cooley operated.

That March day was bleak both outside and inside my hospital room. The doctors continued to give us little hope for Beth Ann's survival. Except for the companionship of despair, loneliness, and cold fear, I was alone. I remember crying out, "God, save my little girl!" For a few minutes I repeated this prayer; then I recalled stories of blue babies and their struggle for life. Selfishly, I amended my petition: "God, take this little girl. You take her before I learn to love her more and possibly be called upon to lose her later. I don't think I could stand that!" But soon I returned to my initial plea, "God, please, save her!" Finally, in sheer confusion and desperation I gasped, "I guess I don't really know what I want — she's yours. Whatever you want is fine with me." In that moment a warm bath of peace and joy engulfed me. I knew that whatever the outcome, it would really be all right.

That time the immediate problem was soon solved. Dr. Cooley came into my room and said, "Congratulations, Carolyn, on your pretty little girl. Take her home and treat her normally." And that's what we did.

Beth Ann is a young woman now and has been a special delight. Recently the doctors asked, "Just how did you manage to raise her to be so pretty and so personable?" Although she still gets less oxygen than normal, Dr. Helen Taussig, the doctor who created the operation, says that this particular surgery was more successful in Beth Ann's case than in any other she has ever seen. But we soon forgot that God had any part in making it so.

During this period I exercised what Gert Behanna calls "bellhop religion." We ask God to come into our lives to carry our bags of problems, our many parcels of pain; then when the problems are resolved, we say, "Thank you very much. We'll call you again some day when we have more luggage too heavy for us to manage alone." Without even a tip or a courteous nod in his direction, I dismissed God when I'd finished with his services.

I believe that God has been inviting me always to "walk with him in his story." On that cold March morning, I faintly heard the words, but I chose to refuse the invitation, and he allowed me to do so. As St. Augustine said, "He who created us without our help will not save us without our consent." I continued to live behind my thick, private insulation.

In April, 1959, Chuck was in South America on a business trip when healthy, robust Carl became ill. The diagnosis was a fatal blood disease.

Tragedy brought sudden darkness; and like the bridesmaid in Jesus' parable, I was caught with an empty lamp and could find no way quickly to replenish it. Indeed, having no oil of faith to light my path, I surely suffered the blackest night of the soul. Terrified by a fear that I had never met before, I was in such quicksand of terror that I could barely function. Some dark, shapeless thing had shattered my insulation, and the shock was almost more than I could bear. I stepped into an unknown land filled with fears and panic; there were no familiar landmarks and many dragons.

During the first week of Carl's hospitalization, an Episcopal minister came to Houston on a preaching mission. Chuck (who had immediately flown home from South America) and I were invited by a friend to attend. We had never heard of Sam Shoemaker, but our friend, Eugenia, suggested that this man might meet a need in our present grim situation. Desperate as we were, we snatched at any morsel offered. We went to hear Sam Shoemaker speak.

His first lecture was on the stream of the Holy Spirit, and I listened intently. In the past, I guess if anyone had asked me if I believed in God (and I can't remember anyone's ever asking),

I would have said that I believed in a God who had created the world and then left us to our own business. Yet here was a man telling me that God wanted to do business with me, that he cared for me, Carolyn, in a personal way. I was not just a miscellaneous small one. I was special! Sam said that when Jesus Christ left his Holy Spirit for us many promises accompanied that gift. He said that the Spirit could comfort, convict, empower, guide, restrain, and even call up the words of Christ. This seemed too incredible to be true! It was as if Sam had taken a razor blade and split open the sky for me! God's Holy Spirit — could such a thing really be true?

We returned every night to hear more. Each evening Sam Shoemaker told us more about God and his Holy Spirit. At the close of the last night's lecture, he suggested that all who were interested form small groups to get together weekly for prayer and Bible study. We joined one of these groups and were helped greatly by other searching people, most of whom were as ignorant as we of the Bible. But God met us with our puny commitment. Eagerly, I read and studied the Bible and any other book that spoke of God and his plan for me. I would take a book with me in the car, and every time the light turned red, I'd grab my book and read. I know this is not the safest procedure, but I had no thought for safety, mine or anyone else's. I was trying to make up for all of those lost years of noninvolvement with God and his world.

I became very interested in reading, or perhaps I should more accurately say, in misreading books on spiritual healing. Misinterpreting passages, I emphasized what would work in my behalf. The doctors had no encouragement for us; so I must look elsewhere. Finally, I fashioned a God according to my need. I even arrived at a formula (those early Hebrews and I were great in searching for formulas!) — if my faith were strong enough (and it most certainly would be!), then my son would be healed. It was as simple as two plus two equals four. My faith plus God's power would equal Carl's total healing. I would accept no alternative. I would never consider saying, "I believe that you can heal [which I do], and I believe that you can perform your miracles [which I do]; I lift this child up to you and ask for special healing — nevertheless, not my will but yours be done in this situation." No, there was no such option open for me. Hadn't I called the "bellhop God" once before? Hadn't he solved the problem? Surely, he would — he must — again! There was to be no prayer of relinquishment this time, no compromise, no suggestion of "God, here is this situation with Carl. I leave it for you. I accept your decision."

I was a frantic, hurting mother who had only a nodding acquaintance with God. In this desperate game, I made the rules. My faith would be strong enough; Carl would be healed. The medical profession would be amazed, and many recruits would be won for God who would surely be glorified in such a transaction. Of course, glorifying God was certainly way down on my list of priorities. For me, Christianity had become a potpourri caldron, boiling and bubbling up. I was frantically choosing only the positive things that applied to me and mine. Chuck never traveled this road, but he allowed me the freedom to do so.

Carl was doing business with God in his own way. For a six-year-old, he possessed an unexplainable knowledge of God's reality. This child had always seemed to have a unique quality, a special spirit, an indescribable sensitiveness. He was physically beautiful, had a brilliant mind and a talent for art, but most of all possessed a gift for loving. Carl showed compassion for all around him. During his three months' illness, he seemed to sense that his time here was to be brief. He talked of God a great deal, and, in our zest to know more of this God of the universe, we too talked about God a great deal those days.

One day Carl and I were modeling with clay. For a design, we needed a big leaf to press into the clay. I went outside in search of one. Since our neighborhood was new, it furnished nothing but young trees with very small leaves. I found no leaf. Carl went outside to the flower bed, reached down, and plucked off a big ribbed leaf from the marvelous hydrangea plant. "Carl," I said, "how did you ever think of that? It's the perfect thing!"

He answered simply, "The Holy Spirit told me."

Recently, Elaine, Carl's playmate, now a lovely young woman, said, "I remember that one day I was frightened, and Carl Huffman told me, 'Elaine, never be afraid. Don't you know that God is always with you?'" While I was busy running around the smorgasboard perifery of God's truth, Carl was grounded in the very center of it!

Carl died. The God I fashioned died, and I died. I no longer wanted to walk in my own story. I surely did not want to walk in God's story, for he had allowed Carl to die. He was no longer worthy to be called God of my life. I did not care what he did with his universe; I wanted no part of that either. I can remember only one crazy thing that I thought I had to be thankful for: At least I was not one of those great, giant tortoises, for I had heard that they lived to be very old. I had already lived much longer than I desired!

2

Land of No Caring

We respond in such different ways to grief and suffering. I never again wanted to speak to the Lord-God of the universe, but Chuck wanted to lay down his life for him. I heard only the screaming, resounding call of grief; Chuck heard the clear call to the ministry. He had felt the sure tap on his shoulder. It would take nothing less than the true God to yoke such an unlikely pair together in service for him.

The agonizing pain of that first year with grief as my constant companion defies description. Not only had I walked onto a strange terrain full of dragons and unidentifiable landmarks, but I had stepped into a land void of color — unless you call black a color. The sky had lost its blue; the grass had lost its green. Everything blended into everything else and ran down the drain into one big blob of paralyzing, screaming, constant suffering and brokenness. O my God, how I hurt! Just don't reach out even to touch me, for every spot represents a raw canker sore of painful madness.

I felt completely trapped on this earth; I didn't know how to escape its boundaries, yet I had no desire to live within them. Suicide — and I considered this option — might only intensify my separation from Carl, create an even deeper chasm between us. Still believing that God had betrayed me, I wanted to do no more business with him. In fact, every time God was mentioned, my stomach muscles tightened, and my throat constricted. Because of great awe, fear, and respect, the ancient Hebrews would not dare to write God's name or call him by name. Because of great anger, pain, and resentment, I chose to delete the name of the Lord-God from my life. How wrong we both were!

There was no bitterness in Chuck, only a desire to serve God and someday be a minister. Chuck was willing for God to transform his pain into creative suffering. From the ashes of Carl's death, he wanted God to create a phoenix of meaning and purpose. He felt that Carl was growing from strength to strength, and he did not want to be left behind. Chuck brought me a beautiful gold cross and chain which I wore about ten days and then yanked off my neck, breaking the clasp. I did not want to wear the cross of Christ! I was carrying too many heavy crosses of my own to be burdened down with one other.

Mine was a stoical grief-work; I kept everything silently within. The only person I really wanted to see those days was Jane. Her son had been killed six months earlier. It was incredible to me that she could still get up in the morning and stumble through a day — any day. If you had looked into my eyes those days, you would have seen the reflection of my somber, dead soul.

Chuck wanted to join the Episcopal church and eventually become an Episcopal clergyman. Remembering my attitude, I am surprised, and still can't understand why, I agreed to join him in becoming an Episcopalian. I had shut Chuck out of my life along with closing the door on God and all others. I can only guess that agreeing to attend confirmation classes might have been a guilty token crust thrown in his direction.

My body attended sessions with fists clenched and arms folded, but my head and heart heard none of the words. I went along until several days before the confirmation itself. Each of us was given a card stating that the signer would try to follow Jesus Christ with all his heart, mind, and soul. I balked! I refused to sign the card. After all, I was not even on speaking terms with God. Surely I could not perpetrate such a flagrant lie!

I hastened to talk to Tom Sumners, rector of St. John the Divine Episcopal Church. Tom and his wife, Doris, had been so good to us during Carl's illness. He was responsible for bringing Sam Shoemaker to Houston; he had held Carl's funeral service. Even in my "land of no caring" I could feel a portion of concern and love for this man who had done so much for me when I was not even a member of his parish.

I told Tom my dilemma. Instead of saying, "Carolyn Huffman, until you can agree to the statement on that card, you must not be confirmed," this wise, loving, gentle man said, "Carolyn, you don't have to sign this card or any other. Just take who you are and where you are right now up to the altar rail; you present that, and let God do the rest." And so I did.

Tom was also important to me in another way. A number of months had passed since Carl's death. Chuck and friends were beginning to be concerned, for my robot soul seemed to be as dead as ever. Chuck asked if I would please have a talk with Tom Sumners. Tom also asked to see me; so I went to his office. I told him that I was still extremely bitter and angry with his God and wanted no part of him. I could not and would not pray. With this, he said, "Carolyn, will you do this for me, not God? Daily will you pray these simple words, 'Lord, help me to love thee more'? Now, you can do that, can't you — for me?" I loved Tom, and so I said, "I will do it for you as long as you know, and I know, and most of all, God knows, that I am not doing it for him!" For almost a year, this was my sole prayer.

Another important element in the rebuilding, reshaping, life-changing process of Carolyn Huffman was the communion service. Chuck and I responded so differently to monster grief. He wanted to talk about Carl, look at his pictures, remember the precious moments; I couldn't bear to speak Carl's name or see his picture. The only time I allowed my heart and mind to rest on Carl's image was at the communion rail. In all my rebellion, I never once doubted that God was, that eternity was, and that Carl still was. There was no question of that and never has been. I knew there was a God. I just resented the manner in which he ran his universe, but in particular, the manner in which he refused to fit his infiniteness into my life-style. It did not bother me so much that he had let other mothers' sons die; that was life's pattern. But when he stepped across my No Trespassing sign, that was something else. He had messed up my life in an unforgivable fashion. And though he was not a God I wanted to do business with, I still believed he was God and was there. In the Episcopal church we accept the doctrine called "communion of the saints." We affirm the Apostles' Creed that Christians in heaven and on earth are united through Christ during Holy Communion. So at the communion rail, for just a few precious moments, I was there, Jesus Christ was there, and Carl was there. I would open the door briefly; then I would return to my pew to lock once again the door to my dead soul.

For months, I barely existed. Between praying daily, "Lord, help me to love thee more," and going to the communion rail for brief moments of freedom, I spent my days in perfunctory activities. I saw to it that Beth Ann had clean clothes, the proper food to eat, and appropriate supervision for a three-year-old, but I gave her none of the special things that sing of motherhood. There were just no songs.

I became pregnant, and I was glad. I am surprised that I even wanted another baby, for my heart still resembled a hard stone. My coloring book still had only black pictures.

Chuck became more and more involved with this God whom he loved. He attended prayer groups and even spoke to groups about the love of God in his life. Well, Chuck could do whatever he wanted as long as he left me alone in my shell. He seemed to be doing well with his life, and I would certainly continue to see to it that he had clean clothes, good food to eat, and the polite phrases due a husband. But I gave him none of the special things that sing of wifehood; again, there were just no songs to sing.

I spent many of those first days and months in my car, driving to nowhere. One phrase crept constantly into my thoughts: "I will never have another happy ——." It might be many things. I will never have another *happy Christmas,* or I will never have another happy *Mother's Day,* or *Halloween,* and so on.

And now, December 10, Carl's seventh birthday, and no Carl. The ringing of the telephone interrupted my black reflections. I picked up the receiver and recognized Rev. Claxton Monro's voice. Chuck had been meeting with him once a week in a small group at St. Stephen's Episcopal Church; especially had he been encouraging Chuck about the ministry. At one time, Claxton had been Sam Shoemaker's assistant. Clax called to speak to Chuck. I told him he was not at home, and then I started crying about Carl. Instead of patting me on the shoulder, so to speak, and saying, "There, there, I am sorry; you have every right to cry; you just go ahead and cry," Claxton did something very different. He gave what Gert Behanna calls "tough love."

Claxton loved me enough not to offer a few plastic bandaids when real surgery was needed to prevent the patient from dying. Trying to save my life, he risked losing my friendship. In love, Clax said, "Carolyn Huffman, you have not given Carl up; you have not relinquished him. Turn him loose. Until you do, you will not move ahead one bit spiritually; if you do, there is no telling what might happen. Turn Carl loose!"

Furious, I hung up the phone and cried all the harder. It was rare in those days for me even to be able to cry. What a cruel man was Claxton Monro! Surely he had no compassion and no heart!

After two days, I found myself listening against my will to the words that would not disappear. "Turn him loose. You haven't relinquished him; Carl never belonged to you in the first place!" I had to accept the fact that Claxton just might be right. So, very quietly, I said, "Lord, I do turn Carl over to you. I release him. He is yours." And I think I scribbled at the end of the prayer, "And me too."

Sitting in the car a few days later, I came to some very realistic (I thought) conclusions: "That's right, Carolyn Huffman, the happy life for you is over, complete. You will never have another happy anything, but you are thirty years old, and think of all the happy years you've had. Some people in this world never have a portion of the happiness you have experienced. Accept the fact that happiness for you is surely over, but see if you can be a good mother, a real mother to Beth Ann, who certainly deserves more than you have been giving her. See if you can be a good wife to Chuck who has certainly been shortchanged. Let this be your life-style from now on. Think of these others."

These words seemed to ring clear and true and reached way down where I lived. So I added this philosophical viewpoint to my "Lord, help me to love thee more," my communion service, and my prayer of relinquishment. I turned the car home from nowhere, sensing momentarily that I might be heading, after all, for somewhere.

3

Do What You Must . . .

Slowly, very slowly, I allowed God to unbind the tightly woven threads of my sorrow. Gradually, I allowed him to take me by the hand and gently lead me into the land of color. My prayer, "Help me to love thee more," so obstinately offered, had begun to bear fruit. I don't know exactly how it happened or when it happened — I only know that it happened. I did love him, a small portion, and wanted to learn to love him more.

My trysts at the communion rail continued, but I found I was able to reflect more easily upon this precious son at other moments too. My relinquishment prayer was the cornerstone in a mosaic that represented my climb back from frenzied nightmare to reality, from a brackish, cloying black, covering me like the sky, to color and breaths of fresh air. My acceptance that truly "I would never be a happy 'anything' again," coupled with my desire to try to give happiness to my child and my husband produced a surprising result. As I concentrated less on myself and more on extending love to others, cupfuls of happiness often spattered up on me from the backwash! I joined a Bible study prayer group and gratefully received the support of fellowship in the body of Christ.

At first I was able only to stumble and limp along in my story. Gradually, I was able to offer to walk with God in his story if it didn't interfere with my plans or desires. Lest you think that the wings of sorrow became faint and finally disappeared completely, let me assure you this was not so. It is not so now, and I suspect it never will be. Reflecting on the loss of his wife, C. S. Lewis states in *A Grief Observed:*

> Getting over it so soon? But the words are ambiguous. To say the patient is getting over it after an operation for appendicitis is one thing; after he's had his leg off it is quite another. After the operation either the wounded stump heals or the man dies. If it heals, the fierce, continuous pain will stop. Presently he'll get back his strength and be able to stump about on his wooden leg. He has "got over it." But he will probably have recurrent pains in the stump all his life, and perhaps pretty bad ones; and he will always be a one-legged man. There will be hardly any moment when he forgets it. Bathing, dressing, sitting down and getting up again, even lying in bed, will all be different. His whole way of life will be changed. All sorts of pleasures and activities that he once took for granted will have to be simply written off. Duties too. At present I am learning to get about on crutches. Perhaps I shall presently be given a wooden leg. But I shall never be a biped again.[1]

People in grief do wonder when they will "get over it." With Lewis, I don't think you ever "get over it." You either "die" or you allow God to transform the suffering into a creative work like wings of the morning after the darkness of the night. For me, this grief-work has so far been a lifetime assignment.

Several months before my third child was born, I dreamt of Carl. He was standing in a field of green, green grass and wore a plain white robe. Across the robe in cut-out letters (similar to the old-fashioned hand-to-hand cut-out paper dolls) was the name *Heather*. He said, "Mama, don't worry about me. I am happy. I am busy — there are so many things to do!"

I awakened with a feeling of great joy as if I had just had a good visit with Carl. I also had the conviction that I was to have a little girl and her name was to be Heather. We did have our little girl, Heather. In no way could she ever replace Carl, but she seems to possess his same essence. It was almost as if God were saying, "I can't return Carl to you, but here is a special little girl with similar qualities." Heather has a sensitive nature: loving and caring seem to come easy for her.

Two years later we were blessed with another daughter. Laura, our elf, has a constant twinkle in her eye, a ready smile on her face, and God's joy in her heart. And so we were five, and my days were busy indeed!

But the "hound of heaven" followed Chuck's every move; my husband continually felt the gentle yet firm tap on his shoulder. Since there was no encouragement from me, he tried to satisfy this hunger in work and study. Chuck had become more and more active in the life of the church, Bible study, and small groups, and he continued to be called upon as speaker to share how God in Christ had become real to him.

Having always wanted to be in business for himself, Chuck readily accepted the proposal of two engineers from Texas Instruments to form an electronics corporation. Perhaps this would answer his need for greater fulfillment. Perhaps this would still the sentinel that continued to whisper, "Come, Chuck, be my minister." I hoped it would choke out forever Chuck's crazy, frightening idea of going to seminary. I had run from two boys in college who had that crazy idea. I wanted no part of it now! But like the proverbial crab grass, it kept cropping up all over. Every time Chuck mentioned the subject, I cried and told him he just wanted to retreat from reality. After all, I reminded him, he had a wife and three children to support. Then I would point out that he was clearly doing great work as a layman in Houston, Texas, that he was needed as God's steward here.

For many people this is true. God calls us to be his people, his stewards in all arenas of life. There are other calls besides a call to the ordained ministry; our task is to heed the Spirit's guidance. But in Chuck's case I objected chiefly because I did not want so drastically to change my own life-style. It was one thing to agree sometimes to "walk in God's story" in Houston, Texas; here, I had my family, my friends, my security, my church, my prayer groups, my beautiful old house near Rice University. My hidden agenda called for living in this house the rest of my life! It was one thing sometimes to allow God to ride in my car with me, but I was not about to be so audacious as to "give him the keys." Who knows where he might take me? After each crying spell, I would sweep seminary under the rug and pretend, for a while, that I did not notice the lump in the carpet that continued to grow and grow.

Sam Shoemaker returned to Houston for another preaching mission. Chuck had corresponded with Sam concerning his call to the ministry. That week they spent much time together, talking of God and his Holy Spirit — of life. We attended every session. Again, we were thrilled as Sam spoke of a powerful yet loving God, a Father who wanted to get involved with his children. He told stories of men in Pittsburgh who had decided to take a chance with this God; he told how God had been faithful and had met them at the point of their greatest need. He spoke of an exciting group of laymen whom he had organized in what he called the Pittsburgh Experiment: these men were reaching out and healing brokenness in the old city of Pittsburgh. "See," thought I, "laymen are desperately needed to do God's work!" Surely, Chuck would come to his senses. Maybe I had found a great ally in Sam Shoemaker!

The next day my friend Katherine called. She had news. She had spent the afternoon with Sam and heard Chuck's story of wanting to go to seminary. She had also heard how I explained it all away. Katherine carefully told me Sam's resounding response. Evidently, with much show of emotion, Sam had pounded the table and said, "When a man truly receives a clear, loud call from God to go into the ordained ministry, nothing but going into the ministry will ever suffice!"

Later on, Sam related this incident in one of his books. My defenses crumbled! I knew that "sweeping Chuck's call under the rug" was no longer the way to handle this problem. I also knew that I could not chance his pointing a finger at me, years down the road, and saying, "If it weren't for you, Carolyn Huffman, I would be a minister in God's church." He had already told me that he needed my support, that he could never do it alone. So, that day when Chuck came in from talking with Claxton Monro and said, "I feel this is something I must do," I cried all the harder. But then I said, "All right, Chuck Huffman, do what you must do to see if you can even get into seminary. I'll do my best to accept it; if you feel that God is really calling you, I ask that he touch me and let me sense that call too." As in so many cases, I learned that God doesn't necessarily change the circumstances, but he changes our attitude toward them. Seminary was the scary unknown. We had to meet the needs of our three children, and I had to face leaving my known support. I might not have been walking at a brisk pace in Houston, but at least I had learned to hobble around slowly with some joy. What might a move such as this hold? I had to face giving up my beautiful home. None of these facts had really changed; yet in relinquishment, I found a new undefinable peace and a new joy.

Chuck started taking action, and you have never seen so many doors open so fast! Chuck believed that the best way to tell if a door was to open was to start rattling the doorknob and "stepping on the automated doormat." God has a difficult time guiding a stationary object and Chuck was moving! Everything fell into place; even our financial worries were taken care of. St. John the Divine wanted to support us for our entire stay at seminary! Chuck was accepted. Eagerly we anticipated September, 1963, and our move to Austin, Texas.

Three weeks before our departure, I went into a small book store owned by a friend of mine. Checking out some lending library books, I casually remarked that I had better read them promptly for we were moving in three weeks. She seemed surprised. I told her of Chuck's decision to go back to school, to seminary, and then I left the shop. Two weeks later I returned to see signs on all of the windows: "Going Out of Business Sale." I entered and said, "You never told me you were going out of business."

She laughed, "I have wanted to do this for years, but I never had the courage. When you told me that Chuck Huffman at his age [he was thirty-seven], and with his responsibilities, could risk such a change, I decided that I could risk one too! I have already sold the shop and have a position at Rice University!" I never heard from her again.

The moving van had gone, and the big house seemed so empty. Chuck told me to take the children to his parents' home around the corner; he would be there in a few minutes after doing one last thing — clean the ashes from the fireplace. Later he came walking into the house around the corner with ashes on his hands and tears streaming down his face. "You so loved that house," he said.

"Chuck Huffman," I answered, "I turned that house loose months ago. I'm not shedding any tears today for that house, and don't you either! Let's head for Austin!"

4

A Sack of Pecans

The first weeks in Austin were scary. Had we really made the right decision? Were we foolish to embark on such a perilous journey at this stage in our lives? Should we have made such a radical change? How would our children adjust? Would we be able to live on our money allotment? And, would I really have to wear dresses from the "mission barrel"? (Little did I dream that I would soon be the proud owner of a beautiful Don Loper, Hattie Carnegie, and Geoffrey Beene, all from the seminary clothing exchange. What a "mission barrel"!)

What would people think? How well I remembered what Chuck and I had thought about our friends, Calton and Janie, who had been in college with us. Calton had a good job in Houston, but a number of years ago, without warning, he had gone to seminary to become an Episcopal minister. This seemingly irresponsible act had concerned Chuck and me. We made statements like, "They always were on the religious side," and "I guess the business world just wasn't for Calton." Since at that time we'd had no encounter with a living Lord who had a story for us to walk in, we thought it incredible that a talented young man with such a promising future should deliberately throw it all away in a foolish act. (Coincidentally, Chuck's first sermon was preached in Calton's church.) I am sure that many people made similar statements about us and wondered about the stability of our decision making.

During those first months, in spite of the initial anxieties that always seem to accompany beginnings, I began to feel a calm reassurance and seemed to sense God's presence in a very real way. Often, it became imperative to interrupt my activity and record my thoughts.

My name is "Hunger."
I stand by the road and watch the people pass.
I look thru the eyes of Christ,
My spirit does groan and ask:
Aren't you hungry for more of me?
You ones who pass me by?
Aren't you hungry for my word, my love?
Don't you know your time does fly?

They call me "Thirst."
I stand by the road and watch the people pass.
I look thru the eyes of Christ and ask:
Aren't you thirsty?
Doesn't your tongue parch for living water I hold?
Don't you want cool refreshment found
When my waters of life enfold?

Recognize me? I'm "Weary."
I stand by the road and watch the people pass.
I look thru the eyes of Christ and ask:
Aren't you weary?
Aren't you tired of shouldering your burden all alone?
Won't you take my Holy Spirit and
Receive help from my throne?

My name is "Hope."
I stand by the road and watch the people pass.
I look thru the eyes of Christ and ask:
Won't you please take this my outstretched hand?
It is I, the son of God, and man
I offer you my life, your life eternal for ever more;
My name is Hope, and I shall ever remain at your door.

And what of me, "Pain"?
I stand by the road and watch the people pass.
I look thru the eyes of Christ and ask:

Don't you hurt for my promises you have cast aside?
Weep for these nail prints and bruises
In my side?

They call me "Forgiveness."
I too stand and watch the people pass.
I look thru the eyes of Christ and ask:
Can't you forgive your brother as I forgive thee?
Can't I ask this of you that you ask of me?

You know me as "Patience."
I stand by the road and watch the people pass.
I look thru the eyes of Christ and ask:
Don't you know you will ne'er have peace until
You come to me?
Must I wait for you thru all eternity?

My name is "Love."
I stand by the road and watch the people pass.
I look thru the eyes of Christ and ask:
Can't you see the loving Father thru me?
Would you give your son, your only one, as he?
Could you love enough to suffer Gethsemane?
My name is Love, the Holy Trinity.

Writing poetry during those first apprehensive months seemed to give me an inner strength. Perhaps the meter wasn't all it was supposed to be, perhaps the theology would not have passed the test of the seminary scholars, but it was a great affirmation of God's continuing hand on my shoulder.

Immediately upon our arrival I tried to find a Bible study group within the seminary community, but no one seemed interested. Most wives were greatly burdened in assuming the role of breadwinner for their families; they had little time or energy left over for anything but answering the loudest, screaming need in their own homes. Some wives were vehemently vocal or stoically silent in their bitterness and discontent over their husband's decision to enter seminary. They, like me several years ago, wanted to have no close relationship with the Lord of the universe.

I did not feel accepted by the seminary community. On my better days, I could remind myself of the "big picture." I could remember the reality of God in my past, and I could trust him with my future. But on other days, my memory blurred, and my trust level registered minus. Although I could believe that God loved me, I often felt hurt and disappointed that so many of the "flesh-faces" at the seminary didn't seem to want to be my friends. In retrospect I imagine my antennae might have been broadcasting, "You don't really want to be my friend, do you?"

But I knew then, as I know now, that for me to function well in this life, I need the weekly support of the Christian fellowship. So I continued to look and finally found a group in the Presbyterian community. This helped bridge the gap between ending one life-style and beginning another. At the Presbyterian seminary I enrolled in a class taught by a giant of a man, Dr. Charles King; to sit at his feet was a privilege. For companionship, I had college friends and family in town. These were happy days; I eagerly anticipated our future.

Seminary life was far more difficult for Chuck than it was for me or for the girls. He faced the challenge of once again being a student. Having received his B.S. in physics in 1949, Chuck had not been challenged by disciplined study in a long time. It was one thing to feel the tap on the shoulder and anticipate standing as a priest at God's altar; it was another thing indeed to face the stark reality of mastering Greek and learning theology. Chuck's background in physics and engineering had been gained at the expense of English, philosophy, foreign languages, and other humanities. Most of the men were much younger than Chuck who was sometimes mistaken for one of the professors.

Friday afternoon of the first week of classes I looked out the window to see a very somber and anxious Chuck crossing the front porch. I braced myself for the bad news he was sure to relate. "Start packing, we might as well go home now; I can never make it!" he said. He had been given the massive assignment of memorizing the entire outlines of St. Matthew's, St. Mark's, and St. Luke's Gospels. For a man of physics and engineering, this seemed an impossible task, one that he was not prepared even to attempt. I calmed him down, and together we composed a memory code of ridiculous sentences. It worked, and he came through with flying colors.

On Chuck's first theology examination, the professor passed out the "blue books" for an essay test. Chuck had studied many hours in preparation, but essay tests were new to this man of science and engineering. After filling only the first page of the blue book, he was through! He had very scientifically and concisely had his say — all on one page. Chuck was shattered when his paper was returned with "D" and a note, "Please write more next time." Chuck learned to fill up many blue books before seminary days were over, but the learning process was not easy.

Equally as frightening as the academic challenge was the challenge to his new-found faith. Evidently, those were strained times for all seminaries. The God Is Dead doctrine was sounding its notes across the land, and when Chuck entered, one of the main advocates of such a doctrine was theology professor at our seminary. The social action emphasis was also prominent during those early days of the sixties. Don't misunderstand. I feel the Christian has no option. He must reach out to the brokenness of God's people, or he counterfeit's Christianity; it just seemed to me that in those days social action was a one-legged stool on which most seminaries sat. The angry young men were heroes; the men who tried to hold fast the traditional faith often found it difficult.

Our own seminary raised high the doctrine of freedom of thought and expression for every man. Every one had the inalienable right to be fairly heard! In policy, this might have been true, but in practice it proved to be a puppet-show parody.

Whenever the seminarians, like Chuck, the ones who were trying to hold fast to the traditional posture, tried to put their "flags of truth" on the bulletin board, they were ignored, torn down, or worse still — ridiculed.

Discovering that God wanted to do business with him had been a life-changing experience for Chuck; now his New Testament professor told him that the Holy Spirit was simply a biblical literary device, helpful in bridging gaps and in explaining some passages. Another professor implied the irrelevance of the Old Testament; he thought it merely an heirloom to be handed down as one would pass on Aunt Minnie's pearls.

Let me hasten to say that seminary today here in Austin is very different from seminary '63. Before, the seminary was concentrating on becoming a graduate school of theology. The mood was disharmony and discord with cynicism toward the institutional and disdain toward traditional values. Now the emphasis is more on preparing the student for the parish ministry — teaching him more about death and dying, and life and living. Just recently I heard Bishop Hines make a plea for better seminary education. He said, "The seminary should be a place where the professor and the student can *meet* God, not just study about him."

Concerned about the climate of the seminary, Chuck wrote to Sam Shoemaker. This was Sam's reply:

> I am glad the book *On Starting Your Ministry* has helped. It is strange the way God has let me be around at times of such importance in your life; you way down in Houston and I up here. I thank God for it, and for the way he is leading and going to use you. Thank God you came into the ministry on the way of an experience, not just an idea.
>
> Devotedly,
> Sam

A few months later on All Saints Day, we received the sad news that Sam Shoemaker had died. Chuck and I sat at the kitchen table and cried. We felt the loss deeply. It helped to write our condolences to Helen Shoemaker. In answering, she sent us a copy of Sam's credo, written shortly before his death:

CREDO

As I sit in the study on a beautiful, cool August afternoon, I look back with many thanks. It has been a great run. I wouldn't have missed it for anything. Much could and should have been better, and I have, by no means, done what I should have done with all that I have been given. But the overall experience of being alive has been a thrilling experience. I believe that death is a doorway to more of it; clearer, cleaner, better, with more of the secret opened than unlocked. I do not feel much confidence in myself as regards all this, for very few have ever "deserved" eternal life. But with Christ's atonement and Him gone on before, I have neither doubt nor fear whether I am left here a brief time or long one. I believe that I shall see Him and know Him, and that eternity will be an endless opportunity to consort with the great souls and the lesser ones who have entered into the freedom of the heavenly city. It is His forgiveness and grace that gives confidence and not merits of our own. But again I say, it's been a great run. I'm thankful for it and for all the people who have helped to make it so, and especially those closest and dearest to me.

Samuel M. Shoemaker[1]

During the first year of seminary, whenever Chuck experienced a spiritual drouth, I would suggest that he confer with Dr. Charles King at the Presbyterian seminary. While taking Dr. King's course, I had heard him tell his senior students that he sensed a lack of the life of the Spirit at the seminary (Presbyterians were having their own problems). That last day of class, he gave an electrifying talk to a group of graduating seniors. He suggested that they might at least *sometimes* nod in the direction of the Holy Spirit! And then he stood even taller and told them, "If you don't have a devotional life and try to be led by God's Holy Spirit, the words you preach will sound like sounding brass and tinkling cymbals."

Chuck always returned from conversations with Dr. King with a steadier step. I would ask, "What did Dr. King say?"

Chuck's answer was, "I can't remember what he said; that's not important. It's what he is and what he stands for; that's the important thing." I would know that for a little while Chuck would once again be feeling strong and firm in his personal faith.

Unfortunately, many of the other seminarians did not have the benefit of such support. With no clear guidance they seemed to grow bitter, cynical, and disillusioned. Not only were they confused about the "faith of their fathers," but they found it difficult indeed to come up with a faith in anything or in any god. I remember a conversation that I had over the breakfast table in our kitchen. The young woman said, "My husband is to graduate in a few months. He and I are spiritually bankrupt; we have nothing to sustain ourselves, much less to give to anyone else; if something doesn't happen in the next few months, I don't know what we will do." I shared my faith with her. I told her about God who wanted to do business with his people. She started to cry and said, "Oh, I didn't know anyone believed like that anymore." During the next few months she withdrew more and more. Her husband graduated, and they went back to the northern part of the country. We never heard from them again.

The first Christmas in seminary was a good one. On Christmas Eve a nice lady from one of the nearby churches rang our doorbell. She gave us a sack of pecans and wished us a Merry Christmas. As we followed her out on the porch to say good-by, she turned and said, "I just want to tell you that I think it's wonderful this great sacrifice you are making."

As she drove away, Chuck and I turned to each other in surprised confusion, and then we began to laugh. Many words could describe those first months at seminary, but *sacrifice* was nowhere in the bundle. More accurate terms would have been *joy,* some *anxiousness,* and whispered, tiptoed *anticipation!* We walked inside to enjoy the pecans.

5

A Very Special Man

In January, 1965, a very special man came into my life. I fell in love with Dr. John Knox who had come to our seminary for one semester as a guest lecturer. He was to return to his own seminary the following fall. John Knox came with many credentials, but I was interested in things far more important than credentials: What of the personal faith and commitment of this man? I decided to audit his course on christology.

On that first class day, in front of the room stood a tall, slender, immaculately dressed man. John Knox, in his middle sixties, had the most alive, compassionate eyes I had ever seen. He had a special joy about him too. He said that he did not know the policy at our seminary concerning starting classes with prayer but that his class would always open with prayer. "Why do I want to do it?" he asked. "Why do I hope that you do not object? Because in prayer we come closer to being together than in any other activity — closer at a deeper level. I covet this sort of relationship with all of you, not just between the old instructor and younger student, but among all of us. Also, when we pray we are, if our prayer is sincere, being entirely open toward God, toward one another in his presence, in touch with the reality which all our religious talk is about, on which all our beliefs are based."

In another seminary class Chuck had whispered an aside to one of his friends concerning the possibility of starting that class with prayer. Overhearing Chuck's remark, the professor said loudly, indignantly, "Mr. Huffman, my whole life is a prayer!" Prayer was never mentioned in that class again.

When John Knox acted as if prayer was an important part of the class period, I sat up straighter and prepared to listen more attentively. To hear him pray and nothing more would have been well worth the effort of attending class. His opening prayer was by Milner White, and later I had him write it down for me.

> Govern our speech, O Word of God, that all our talk, both light and grave, and all the common converse of the day may yet belong to holiness, and may not drown the inward voice which with all the company of heaven would be praising Thee, world without end. Amen.

One knew that John Knox was on speaking terms with the God of the universe and had been doing business with him for a long time! I discovered later that not only was he a man who believed in the importance and power of prayer, but also in the Holy Spirit, in the reality of Jesus Christ, and in a holy doctrine of the church. This was to be a two-hour class with a fifteen-minute coffee break. At the coffee break that first day, I heard a senior say, "I have heard more about Jesus Christ in this one hour than in all the rest of my seminary classes put together!" Had I known that day how very important John Knox would become to Chuck and to me, I would have been shouting more loudly than that senior!

Many of us think of great men as being very busy, sitting on isolated center stages glancing at life as it passes. We might picture them much too involved in handling greatness ever to consider stepping down and marching around with us other plain folk. I do not know about other great men, but I do know that this is not John Knox's life-style. He chooses, even makes a great effort, to get involved with all of God's children in all arenas. I am reminded of Dr. Suess's book, *Horton Hears A*

Who. In this book, Horton, the elephant, keeps insisting loudly and firmly, "a person's a person no matter how small." Daily, Dr. Knox acted out this truth in his life.

John Knox initiated several firsts at our seminary. For one thing he made calls on all of the students. Since this was not seminary policy and since he was to be in Austin for only four months, he was investing energy and time in students whom he might never see again! We all loved it! The only answer was that he cared for each of us. We were all special to him. Obviously, he wanted to be more to us than professor; he wanted to be pastor as well.

On Easter morning Chuck was to leave very early to drive to his faraway church assignment. How surprised we were when Dr. Knox appeared on the doorstep at 6:30 A.M. to accompany him. He did not want Chuck to make the long drive alone.

Another incident showing the depth of Dr. Knox's caring occurred several years later. It was a beautiful spring afternoon in Austin, and I was very busy being mother to my three girls. The telephone rang. It was John Knox. I had told him earlier that I intended to audit his course on Romans. He started the conversation somewhat like this, "Carolyn, tomorrow I must tell the seminary when I would prefer to have my class on Romans scheduled; now, I know how busy you must be in caring for your three little girls. I understand how difficult it will probably be for you to arrange a time to attend my class. Which day would be better for you?"

Taken back by the consideration of this great, gentle man, I gasped, "Why, Dr. Knox, you schedule your class whenever you choose, and I will be there!"

He continued, "Carolyn, which would be easier for you, a one-hour class twice a week or a two-hour class once a week?"

I replied, "Since I have to get a babysitter, a two-hour class once a week would work out much better for me."

"Now, what about Thursday?" he said, I told him that Thursday would be just great. We chatted a little while longer, and then he said good-by. I do not doubt he had similar conversations with other prospective class members, but it was no surprise to me to read the posted class schedule:

> Dr. John Knox's class on Romans will be held Thursday afternoons from 2:00 until 4:00.

"A person's a person no matter how small."

At this time an atmosphere of hostility pervaded the seminary environment. Students disagreed heatedly over the doctrines of the faith. There were differences and discord between professor and professor, between students and professors, between husbands and wives, between the bishops and the seminary, even between the community and the seminary. However, everybody agreed on one thing — John Knox. From dean to janitor, all sensed his greatness and his love.

One day Dr. Knox called me into his office and asked if I was good at keeping secrets. I told him I could be trusted. Then, with a twinkle in his eye, he divulged the good news. He was to return to his seminary to finish one more year; then he was coming back to our seminary as full-time professor. That was wonderful news. Because of his excellent grades, Chuck had been asked to enter the graduate program. Since several people had encouraged him, including his bishop, Chuck had made the decision to stay in school an extra year. This meant that we would still be in Austin when John returned!

We corresponded for a year. When John came back for the September term, I signed up to audit his New Testament course which was offered to first-year seminarians. Until I sat as student under this great Christian scholar, I did not realize how bound and narrow my images and views of Christianity really were. I had been so afraid that someone or some idea might dissolve my undergirding of faith that I had tightly confined my understanding and my outreach. I had kept the windows and doors of my mind securely locked. There was not much stretching room until John Knox walked into my life and into my heart. His gentle yet breathtaking teaching enabled me freely to unlock the latches, throw open wide the door, raise high the windows, and beckon in "truth!" John Knox, aware of each new student's possible anxieties, spent three class periods offering and explicating the core of the faith — deep belief in God, in his son Jesus Christ, and in the power of the Holy Spirit. Once these important guidelines had been established, we were free to hear what else he had to say. When the semester was over, I heard a seminarian remark, "Oh, Dr. Knox, I was so afraid that you were going to take away my faith, but you didn't." In his kindly wisdom he answered, "Never be afraid of truth."

It wasn't so much what John *said* (although I learned much of value), it was more what he was. In his presence I wanted my goals to be a little higher, my thoughts to be a little kinder, and my love to be more embracing and more tolerant. It wasn't just I; everyone seemed to stand a little taller when John was around. One day in class he spoke about the reality of the Holy Spirit for Paul. "The Spirit was real for Paul," he said, "and is really there for us if we are wise enough to be naive enough to recognize it." Not only had John Knox been wise enough to be naive enough to recognize God's Spirit, he had allowed this Spirit to indwell him in a mighty way.

Had I been satified with walking in "God's story" in Houston, Texas, my life might never have touched the life of John Knox! John and his wife, Lois, have immeasurably enriched and blessed Chuck and me.

6

The Power of the Personal

In spring 1966 Chuck received his B.D. from seminary, and a month later was ordained to the diaco-
nate. Before continuing work for the master's degree, we
decided to take a trip. We attended Agnes Sanford's School of
Pastoral Care in Massachusetts. This particular session was
for clergymen and their wives. Similar sessions had been very
meaningful to several of our friends, and this one proved to be
so for us.

On our return trip, Mrs. Sanford invited us to have dinner
in her New England home, a fascinating old house. Chuck and
I were intrigued by some small slits in the rooms. Mrs. Sanford
explained that Americans long ago poured boiling water
through these slits onto attacking Indians below. Then she
took us out back and showed us the little house where she
wrote. As I remember, it was one austere room, containing a
very old table and a small, straight-back chair. I think there
were also an old rocker and a smaller table and a lamp. The
environment had been stripped to insure maximum concentra-
tion; there was no clutter to disturb the thought process of
creativity.

As I look around my own writing station, I'm forced to
laugh at the contrast! First, I have to clear my children's school
notes from the typewriter, hoping they've not used my last
sheet of paper. Then I shove aside the freshly folded clothes

and sit down between the ironing board and the sewing machine. Presently our dogs are battling woodticks, and one little lost fellow has just strolled across my paper. Surely, since God is not a god of formulas or rigid patterns, he can use even disorganized people like me with disheveled writing rooms!

We bade Mrs. Sanford good-by and headed home to begin the final year of seminary. Besides graduate study, Chuck was to work part time at St. David's Episcopal Church, the grand old beautiful church in downtown Austin. Charles Sumners (Tom Sumners' twin brother) had been rector there for many years, including the time Chuck attended the University of Texas and sang in St. David's choir! I'm certain that no one then could have convinced Chuck, an agnostic physics major, that one day he would serve as priest at that very altar. Truly God's paths and his adventures are far more exciting, breathtaking, and fulfilling than anything we could ever scrape together on our own initiative!

June 6, 1967, Chuck was ordained to the priesthood. St. David's was filled with dear ones who had come to witness this glorious day and wish Chuck Godspeed. And though Chuck did not hear God's booming voice or even his whispered words, "Well done, my good and faithful servant!" he felt that truly he was walking in God's story. Shortly after his ordination, Chuck was called to be a full-time assistant at St. David's. He was on his way, ready to begin his ministry and to try in some small way to fulfill the covenant that had begun many years ago with the death of one small boy.

About this time another important person walked into our lives — Keith Miller. Keith, formerly the director of Laity Lodge, a retreat center outside of Kerrville, Texas, had just published his first book, *The Taste of New Wine,* and had moved to Austin to pursue a graduate degree in psychology. Keith, Mary Allen, and their three girls joined St. David's Church. That was a fortunate day for the Huffmans and for the people in the parish, for our friendship with Keith and Mary

Allen became one of those special, indescribable relationships. It was grounded in the Lord Jesus Christ. With Jesus as common denominator, Lord of our lives, we shared many of the spilled-over blessings, including Sam Shoemaker's influence.

In his writing, in his speaking, and in his life Keith Miller stresses the power of the personal. Before Chuck went to seminary and was forced to "tunnel underground" to survive the institutional dragons, he too had stressed the power of the personal. Many times in Houston Claxton Monro had Chuck on his feet telling what God had done in his life. Now, after four years of academic environment, of experiencing aloneness in his faith position, Chuck was gun-shy. His spontaneous approach in sharing the faith had been put in wraps, but Keith Miller was the perfect catalyst to help Chuck shed these crusty wraps and learn to breathe more freely!

At St. David's, Keith taught a weekly adult Sunday school class. People from all over Austin came to hear about the power of the personal, about the risk of being vulnerable in the hope of reaching out and touching someone else's brokenness. Keith talked about a God who wanted to be involved with his people!

One Sunday Keith was to be absent; he said to Chuck, "Will you take my adult class next Sunday? And why don't you tell what God has done in your life?" Chuck agreed to take the class but rejected the idea of sharing the story of his personal spiritual pilgrimage. That sort of thing might have been acceptable in his preseminary, prepriesthood days, but now things were different. After all, he *was* ordained. He had a certain image to uphold, a certain strength to present; might not this vulnerable way of speaking jeopardize his reputation as a minister? Wouldn't he chance criticism from the people? No, it was too risky; he chose to present a very scholarly paper instead.

The next month Keith found that he had to be away again. "Chuck, will you take my class? And — why don't you witness?" Again Chuck ignored this injunction and presented another scholarly dissertation.

In the month to follow, Keith had to be absent one more time. "Chuck, why don't you speak about the power of God in your life?" Either Chuck had run out of excuses, or theological papers, or perhaps he felt the conviction of God's Holy Spirit, but he decided to risk it! He would tell his story. The next Sunday arrived bright and warm, and a large crowd gathered in the adult classroom. Chuck was unaware that Keith had a small group of seminarians praying for him in this venture. They too were waiting anxiously to see if the risk would prove too costly.

Very unemotionally, very simply, Chuck told how he came into the ministry, how he encountered the God who wanted to do business with him. When he finished, there was a pregnant hush across the room; then the people began to stir. Lois Knox came up to Chuck and told him how meaningful the story had been to her. She said that John had wanted to come up also, but he was so touched that he could not talk about it yet. To think that Chuck had been insecure in speaking personally because of his own status as priest and theologian, yet the very power of the personal coupled with God's spirit had reached out and touched the heart of a New Testament scholar!

A young woman touched Chuck on the shoulder. "My name is Nell. I thought your face looked familiar. After hearing your story, I know now where I saw you; we were at Texas Children's Hospital with our little girl when you were there with Carl. Our little girl died seven years ago." That night we saw Nell again at a meeting. Evidently, she had been thinking about Chuck's story, for she spoke to him again: "You have done something creative with your suffering over your son's death. I cannot say the same of my life." It seemed that Nell was living in that cold, black, bitter, hellish world that I still remembered so well. She even had the same dead, robot eyes. Joy was a stranger to her.

Chuck said, "Nell, I am going to pass on to you what a pastor, Claxton Monro, asked Carolyn years ago. Have you turned your daughter loose? Have you relinquished her? Have you really given her up?" The conversation was over. We all went home.

Two days later Nell called me. She said, "Let me tell you what has happened! When I drove home from the meeting, Chuck's questions haunted me. Other people had said similar things to me, but I could always respond, 'You don't understand; you have never lost a child.' I could not say these things to Chuck Huffman. For the first time I had been backed into a corner and had to listen! Hadn't I given her up? Surely I had turned her loose! Hadn't I? Hadn't I? The next morning I cried, and I cried, then I got down on my knees and said something like, 'I do relinquish Susan; I give her up. I turn her loose, and you can take me too.' Well, do you know that my life has been gray for years? For the first time in ages I saw color! Driving my little boy to school this morning, I really saw the flowers and the trees and the sky! And I want to thank you and Chuck!"

Three months later Nell stood in Keith's class to tell the story of how she had traveled from the land of black to the land of vibrant color! There was a new joy in her face; her dead, unresponsive eyes were now alive and shining!

And the prayer group seminarians had anxiously wondered if the risk would be too costly!

7

The Mount of Transfiguration

The next few years were thrilling, happy times. My life was filled with such a rainbow of bright color that the radiance almost blinded me. Not only was I walking in God's story, I was skipping!

Life was full. I took additional courses at the seminary, continuing to learn more of the New Testament. Then, feeling as if I should broaden my base of biblical knowledge, I signed up for Dr. Jim Wharton's Old Testament course. I expected it to be very dry and very boring and proceeded to tell Dr. Wharton on the first day of class that, for me, this course would be strictly a discipline, a duty. I admitted to knowing absolutely nothing about the Old Testament. Enthusiastically he responded, "Are you in for a treat! Are you in for an exciting time! I am so glad that you know nothing of the Old Testament, for you bring with you no false conceptions." Dr. Wharton acted as if he was preparing to dish up strawberry shortcake, while I anticipated a dose of medicine! Still unconvinced, I sat down to begin my discipline.

Was I in for a surprise! Dr. Wharton began to unravel a tale that would challenge the suspense and adventure of any Star Trek episode! And the very God of the universe was the central figure! Jim Wharton said as Sam Shoemaker had said, "Here is a God who wants to be involved with his people; he demands not so much to be understood, but met. Thousands of years ago he was giving the same invitation, 'Come walk with me in my story.' " I learned that throughout their history God was really saying to the Hebrew people (and says to us today), "I don't ask you to understand me; I only ask you to be obedient, to walk with me in my story, and I will give you your lines one at a time." Dr. Wharton said that the main emphasis in the Old Testament was not the Hebrew people and their search for God, but the one they called Lord and his search for them. He said that each "now" moment is a present new reality under Yahweh, and that moment is always a test of relationship. The Lord is not much interested in how you "read your part," but in how you relate now. No one can ever comprehend this God who is always a total surprise and demands further pilgrimage. The important thing is not whether we describe him correctly, but whether we live with him obediently. He is always subject, never object. Neither the Jews nor the Christians fully comprehend God.

During this course I labeled the dismissal bell as "ultimate intruder" and anxiously anticipated every class period. At the end of the semester I was almost sorry that I was not a Jew! I repeated the course the next year. Discipline, indeed!

Besides seminary classes, my life was full in other exciting ventures. Once a week I met with some Christian women in a Bible study sharing group. I also helped lead a young women's group at St. David's Church. Through this experience I became acquainted with others who, like the old Chuck and Carolyn Huffman, were unaware of the power of God's Holy Spirit. One day a friend and I were trying to point to the reality of God in our own lives. I said something like, "Hey, God is real! And he wants to do business with you! His Holy Spirit is real!" When I finished, there was a brief silence, and then a sophisticated young woman sitting at the end of the table began to speak, very distinctly and very glibly: "And did you have imaginary playmates too when you were young?"

What a put-down! After the meeting, I raced into Chuck's office, shut the door, and quietly exploded! "I'm not going back! Those girls really aren't interested in what I have to say about my faith, anyway. I'm much older than they are, and it seems silly, senseless, and a waste of time for me to go back."

Chuck replied: "Carolyn, I really think that you should go back. Someone needs to sound a clear true note." So I returned month after month, but I could not see that any great things were being settled for God's sake.

Several years later I received the following letter from the outspoken young woman:

> I have been thinking about you recently and have come to see that I owe you a letter of apology and thanks. When you were speaking to us there in the women's group, you must have thought my ears were chinked up with caliche mud! I distinctly recall telling the group that the Holy Spirit sounded like an imaginary playmate. That must've grieved you, and I am truly sorry. How wonderful, how real he is! Not long ago I submitted my life to Jesus. Immediately, to my astonishment, I was baptized in the Holy Spirit! It was and continues to be the most joy-filled experience of my life. Till then I'd only had flitting glimpses of Jehovah's power. And little did I guess in the naievte of worldliness, the reality of the "roaring lion." How differently the world now appears. And I praise the Lord for your early witness.

Weekly Chuck and I attended a couples' group led by Keith Miller. Since there were only fourteen of us, the relationships became close and grew in depth. We had certain disciplines and were always trying different prayer experiments. In one particular assignment, Keith suggested that each of us have pencil and paper close by during our daily quiet time. We were to ask God to bring to mind any person or persons he would have us call or visit. We were to write down the names and act upon it. I did as Keith had requested, and immediately a name rushed into my thinking. I gasped loudly, "Oh, no, Lord, not her!" I had heard that this particular woman and her husband were very critical of any emphasis on the power of the personal. She attended our church, but we were polls apart in our thinking. I dreaded the thought of a visit with her. I did not go.

The next Thursday night everyone reported the results of his or her experiment. With the exception of one other girl and myself, every member of the group had thought of specific names and had obediently followed through. After the meeting, the other girl said, "Carolyn, I will pray for you to go see your person, and you pray for me." We made a covenant, but that week I still refused to visit my lady.

At the next meeting, my friend reported victory, but I had to report failure, I chose to dismiss the whole issue from my mind.

Sunday morning arrived with its usual chaotic rush of getting the girls and myself dressed for church. Chuck had left hours ago for the earlier service. With the usual scream of, "Hurry, we are going to be late!" we dashed out the door and started driving toward the church. We had not gone too many miles before I heard the bump, bump, bump, heralding a flat tire! When I pulled over to the side and stepped out to survey the situation, I realized with amazement just where I had stopped — smack in front of my lady's house!

"Now, Lord," I said, "did you really have to go to that much trouble just to get me to visit her? She will most probably be at church anyway." Slowly I walked up the path and rang the doorbell. My "lady" answered. Since she was wearing a hat, I inwardly whispered, "See, she is on her way to church. This is no time for a visit!" Instead, she graciously asked me to come inside and said that she had decided to go to early church that morning and had just come home. Her morning was free! When I called the service station, I was not at all surprised to hear that it would be at least an hour before someone would be free to come fix my tire. I was trapped.

I wish I could say that the visit was profound, or even meaningful, but it wasn't. It was pleasant, but I cannot recall one important comment, nor can I point to any significant result emerging from that encounter. No shiny success trophy was carried home that day. If that particular visit hosted any great merit, I was never made aware of it.

I once heard Donn Moomaw say that God doesn't call us to be successful; he only calls us to be faithful. I reminded myself that success or failure is not the measuring rod for the Christian adventure. But the episode was important to me, for it was a new confirmation of God's hand on my shoulder.

I arrived early at our next meeting and gleefully watched the group gasp as I told my story. No one suggested that my experience was mere coincidence.

In those days I consumed an enormous diet of spiritual food. Not only did I have my seminary classes and small groups, but I had the privilege of attending St. David's Church every Sunday. As a seminary professor once said, "Charles Sumners preaches every sermon as if it might be his last." The Holy Spirit was moving mightily in that old church on the hill!

Balance is imperative in the spiritual life of a Christian. Often I unknowingly emphasize one aspect at the expense of another. One of the promises of the Holy Spirit is "I will convict you," and he is faithful to his word. I discovered one of my hidden bundles of neglect one morning as I was driving my three daughters to school. In response to one of the girl's remarks, I said, "Well, everyone can't have a Paul of Damascus road experience." In chorus they questioned: Paul of what? Who is Paul? What's a Damascus road? A stab of guilt pierced my being! My own children did not know who Paul was! Here I had been feasting at the tables of seminary and study groups, had even taught some groups, and my own children were starving! Only the day before, I had read that Timothy's mother, Eunice, was steadfast in teaching him the ways of the faith. I could not believe that my own children did not know about Paul, about Saul of Tarsus, about his overwhelming experience on the road to Damascus. Immediately I told them the story.

That day when I picked them up at school, I said, "I have an apology to make. I have been going to seminary, studying the Bible, even teaching classes on the Bible, and yet I have neglected to share this great news with you. You have been shortchanged. Please forgive me." They tumbled forth words to assure me of my immediate forgiveness, and then I continued, "I have decided that every morning on the way to school we will have a Bible lesson [I wanted to be realistic in finding a time that they would not resent and a time that I could always honor]."

The girls acted very excited and said, "Let's start tomorrow." Since I had just finished reading the Book of Esther, I told them that story first. They were rapt with attention as I described the beautiful, courageous Esther who, at the risk of her own life, presented herself to the king, telling him that she was really a Jewess and pleading for the life of her people. I also related that Esther had asked her people to fast and pray for her before she made her plea to the king. I had to define the word *fast* for Laura. At the end I said, "Be thinking about what lesson we might learn from this story."

Seven-year-old Laura immediately blurted out, "I learned one thing: If you are a Jew, keep your mouth shut!" Though that wasn't the lesson I anticipated, I consoled myself with "at least the child listened to the story."

That afternoon a bubbling Laura crawled into the car. "Guess what, mama? The teacher read a story about a little Indian boy who went into the woods to fast. The teacher asked if anyone in the room knew what the word *fast* meant, and I was the only one who raised my hand; then the teacher said, 'Oh, Laura, I expected *you* to know, but doesn't anyone else know?' " Since no one else knew, Laura shared her new knowledge with the class. I had to chuckle, for if my child had been asked the question the day before, she would not have known either!

For the rest of the year, we continued telling Bible stories. I remember what a visiting professor had said in class one day: Giving our children so little to "call up" is an indictment of Christianity. You can't "call up" from a vacuum. I need to be reminded of this often, for I struggle constantly to keep from shortchanging those nearest and dearest to me.

With all these bonuses, I truly skipped along in God's story! My spiritual needs were being met, and so were my other needs. Chuck and I bought a beautiful old home in the Tarrytown section of Austin, and Ida Mae, my maid and dear friend, helped me once a week. Chuck was comfortable and happy in his ministry at St. David's Church. The people loved and supported him, and he felt it a privilege to work with Charles and Keith. Renewal was breaking forth. And every fall we were able to see the Texas Longhorns play football. In a small way I sensed how Peter must have felt on the Mount of Transfiguration when he said: "Master, it is good for us to be here: and let us make three tabernacles; one for thee, and one for Moses, and one for Elias" (Mark 9:5). I was certainly willing to build lasting tabernacles in Austin, Texas. Yes, Christianity was exciting business! "Lord, I will walk with you in your story — *in Austin, Texas,* forever. Here am I; send me just about anywhere you choose — *in Austin, Texas!"*

8

Getting in the Wheelbarrow

Studying voraciously, I continued to learn more and more about the God of the universe. I absorbed this knowledge like a sponge and unselfishly and freely would share it — as long as the group was small enough. Unhesitatingly, if I felt the occasion called for it, I would even share over a cup of coffee my new life in Christ Jesus. But — whenever I was asked to speak before a large group of people, I would clearly and unequivocally say no! That might be all right for some Christians, but it was not my cup of tea. While I continued to be steadfastly firm in my belief in the promises of God's Holy Spirit and declared, "I *do* believe he can use me as his instrument, can guide me, empower me, sustain me, comfort me, give to me a wisdom beyond my own wisdom," I was just as steadfastly firm in refusing to speak before large crowds.

One day, with a stabbing awareness, I realized that I was saying one thing with my lips and doing another with my life. Confronted by the truth, I was under conviction. I recalled the story of a high-wire aerialist who was superior in his art. Daily he practiced pushing an empty wheelbarrow across a thin wire. As he became more skillful, he placed bricks in his wheelbarrow. He boasted that one day he would attempt this feat across Niagara Falls! The aerialist had a good friend who deeply believed in the aerialist's skill and encouraged him. Finally, the day of the Niagara Falls feat arrived. The friend kept encouraging the aerialist by saying over and over again, "I believe you can do it! I *know* you can do it." Then the aerialist turned to his good friend and said, "Fine then, you get in the wheelbarrow!"

I saw myself mirrored clearly in this story. I had been saying that I believed in God's power to use me, that I believed in his faithfulness, but I very carefully stayed out of the wheelbarrow. I suppose I mostly trusted God in the areas that I could confidently handle myself. Facing stark reality, I came to a very important fork in my spiritual road. I knew I would have to act on what I had been telling others or keep silent. Dare I risk climbing into the "barrow"? Refusing seemed the more costly act; so I hesitatingly climbed aboard. I knew that the next time someone asked me to speak before a large group, unless there was an honest reason, I would have to whisper yes.

As I sat shaking in the wheelbarrow, I selfishly hoped it would be a long time before I heard the invitation, "Will you come speak?" I was not anxious to start across the high wire! My rather frightened anticipation didn't last long. Chuck and I were spending a rare lazy afternoon when the telephone rang. Chuck answered it, and I overheard him say, "I'll be happy to speak, but I doubt that Carolyn will; she doesn't do that sort of thing, you know, but I will ask her."

Keith Miller had been asked to conduct a three-day renewal conference in a large Episcopal church in Corpus Christi. He was taking three couples with him as a team. One couple would speak each night, and Keith wanted Chuck and me to speak the second evening. As Chuck told me about the invitation, I felt my wheelbarrow begin to shake. I was about to be off across that wire over the abyss!

We arrived in Corpus Christi late Sunday afternoon, and I was already feeling very apprehensive. I had assumed that the conference would be held in the informal parish hall; however, when I arrived that night, much to my horror, I discovered that the meeting was to take place in the very large, imposing, beautiful sanctuary! The young priest in charge was skittish about "renewal in the church," so these three days were to be done "decently and in order" with the Episcopal service of evening prayer preceding each program.

The first night I saw my friend, Paul, climb into the pulpit and begin to speak, and I almost suffered cardiac arrest. In anticipation of being "on stage" the next night, I sat in a puddle of fear. Vividly I recalled a similar experience from my high-school days. In a drama class presentation for assembly, I had confidently begun to recite my speech when my mind went completely blank. The drama teacher clearly gave me my next line, but no words were forthcoming. Somehow I was powerless to get the message from my brain to my speaking apparatus. My good friend was standing next to me. After an eternity of eternities, she finally penetrated my comatose state; with her help, I perfunctorily gasped forth my words. I never went on stage again. As I looked at Paul, I wondered if history was about to repeat itself the following night.

After the service, I dashed up to Keith and said, "We are not going to meet in the sanctuary tomorrow night are we?" But Keith said yes. He explained that the pastor had insisted on certain things and then added, "Don't worry, Carolyn, I probably made many of these people angry tonight by some of the things I said. Most likely they'll not be back tomorrow, and you'll have an empty church." His words did not allay my fears.

We were staying with our friends, Jim and Betty Jo. I told them of my desperate fright. Betty Jo had taught speech at the University of Texas; so that evening she gave me a crash course on how to speak effectively. I was still frightened. I called my mother in San Antonio to remind her to pray for me. Mother's prayers often seem to have a way of being answered in amazing fashion. She assured me she was praying for me and that she had a good feeling about my talk. "I had a vivid dream about you last night," she said. "It was announced on the radio and written in all the newspapers that you had been elevated to the Order of the North Star Ott; only four other people in the whole world share this honor."

I said, "Mother, *what* is a North Star Ott?"

She laughed and said, "I don't know, but I have the feeling that it's something good and very special!" She prayed for me over the phone, and then she said good night.

I wish I could report that the next morning I felt that "peace that passes all understanding," that I knew God was going to guide me and empower me in a mighty way at the microphone. Not so! I felt even more scared than I had been the night before! I was sick at my stomach and had a touch of diarrhea. For lunch, I was able to eat one boiled shrimp; nothing else could slither down my tightly constricted throat.

Late that afternoon the team members met for dinner. By this time it was obvious to everyone how petrified I really was. I didn't even pretend to take a plate. I'm sure Keith himself was beginning to feel a little apprehensive about my evening's performance. Mercifully he did not know of my high-school fiasco! Before leaving for the church, we had a circle of prayer. Each member prayed for the conference and then offered an extra plea, "And, Lord, please help Carolyn." No one was worried about Chuck or Keith. When we arrived at the church, I saw that Keith's prophecy had been in great error. Instead of an empty sanctuary there was standing room only! As I walked toward the back of the beautiful old building, I thought, "Dear God, what am I doing in this rickety old wheelbarrow anyway?"

Chuck, Keith, and I took our places in the choir area. Evening prayer began. The young clergyman read the appointed psalm. I listened, hoping to hear something that would stop my shakes, and then those special words came thundering across my soul: "The testimony of the Lord is sure, making wise the simple" (Psa. 19:7). Wow, I thought, I'm going to take

God at his word. This is surely his testimony, for I wouldn't be here otherwise, and I am certainly his simple! He had just better give me that wisdom he talks about! I am going to expect him to do just that! As if someone had walked in and put a cloak around my shivering shoulders and soul, I began to feel calm and sure. I heard the closing words of the psalm, "Let the words of my mouth and the meditation of my heart be acceptable in thy sight, O Lord, my rock and my redeemer." Keith spoke briefly and then introduced me.

Calmly I walked up to the microphone and began to speak. I even started out by joking about mother's dream. I told the people that I had been afraid of them, but after all, I was a member of the Order of the North Star Ott, so what did I really have to fear? Then I told them about this God who wanted to do business with me and with them. I used no notes; my voice was steady.

Afterward, Betty Jo rushed up and said, "Carolyn Huffman, I'm furious with you! Last night I so worried about you that I even tried to teach you more about public speaking. I have worried about you all day, for you were so desperately frightened. You just spoke as if you'd been doing it for years!"

My wheelbarrow had started moving, and my God was faithful.

9

Not Me, God

In July, 1969, Chuck and I took our yearly vacation trip to Laity Lodge, another one of those beautiful Christian bonuses. When Keith Miller left, our friend Bill Cody became director. Every summer we expectantly wondered what pot of gold awaited us, for each year we found new riches. The physical plant itself is breathtakingly beautiful, the fellowship indescribable, and the resource teachers always exceptional. Eulalia's cooking alone would make the trip well worth the venture.

We always dreaded the last Saturday breakfast at Laity, for this meant it was time to say good-by, to leave the "mount," and to prepare for reentry into the valley of everyday living. Saturday morning 1969 was no exception. Wistfully thinking that it would be another year before I could again bask in the renewal stream of Laity Lodge, I climbed into the car. We had gone only a few miles before Chuck gently dropped his explosive: "Carolyn, I read a book last night — *Not Me, God,* by Sherwood Wirt — and I saw a graphic picture of myself. I have been so happy and so comfortable with my life in Austin that it would almost take something as dramatic as a 'burning bush' to lead me in another direction. Ashamedly, I realize that it has been over a year since I even considered saying, 'Lord, where would you have me go in ministry for you?' I've prayed about it, and I have the conviction that my ministry as an assistant at St. David's Church is coming to an end. I feel I'm being called to another ministry. I have no hint as to the shape that ministry might take or the place it might be. I have said, 'Lord, I am willing to go wherever you would have me go and do whatever you would have me do.' I just thought you should know about it."

My reentry was accelerated tenfold! Were we really to leave Austin? Even to consider the possibility was painful. Hadn't I told God that I would gladly walk in his story — in Austin, Texas? Hadn't I even shown him that having Austin as my base, I could sometimes even get into the wheelbarrow elsewhere? A move would mean no more seminary classes, no more Keith Miller groups, no more St. David's Church. Then I remembered: Sometimes God only asks us to be *willing* to do something for him, but he never actually makes the request. Perhaps this would be that kind of bank account. I would hand him my check, but maybe he would never cash it! For the present, I decided to dismiss this whole tangled web of thinking. But, as I glanced over at Chuck, I sensed that this was no token decision made in the backwash of Laity Lodge inspiration. *Not Me, God* had obviously made a profound impression on Chuck. It had been the catalyst to cause him to focus on some uncomfortable truths in his life. He was dead serious about the possibility of these being omega days at St. David's. As we drove into our driveway, I saw anew our old, white, two-story house. We had recently added a family room and a spiral staircase, a special delight to our girls. We all loved this old house. We had mastered the leave-taking in Houston; I guess we could do it again.

Weeks went by with no reference to a possible change in our life. Chuck told Keith, Charles, and several others of his conviction. Then he told his bishop. Several calls came from other Texas churches. Chuck would consider each situation, and each time he would say, "This doesn't seem right for me," and I would breathe a little easier. After all, something else *could* open up in Austin.

Chuck and Keith and many others in the parish had been working on a renewal weekend for St. David's. Many months of prayer and preparation had gone into the planning of this Venture in Faith. Chuck told me that he had prayed, "Lord, I will leave here when you choose, but if possible, I would love to be here to support the Venture in Faith weekend." And so, except for the occasional times when Chuck considered a specific call, our life went on as usual.

No, that's really not true! The shadow of possible departure was always close at hand when I made decisions. My living room curtains were old and dirty; with one more washing they would disintegrate like a box of tissue. If we were to leave, I did not want the expense of replacing them, so they limply remained at the windows and glared down at me. And the same with the flowerbeds. If we were not going to be here to enjoy them, I hated to buy costly plants. When someone asked, "Will you have the ladies Christmas party?" I said no and mumbled some inane excuse. I did not have the courage to tell the woman my real reason. Would she understand it if I said, "You see God is calling Chuck to an unknown task, in an unknown place, at an unknown time"? Christmas came and went, and we were still sitting in our beautiful white house with the spiral staircase. We seemed no closer to a move than we had been in July. In this jet age of the twentieth century, the God of the universe often moves at a snail's pace!

With January came the long awaited Venture in Faith. Bruce Larson, Heidi Frost, Keith Miller, and many other Christians participated. In his or her own way each person pointed over the shoulder to the one he or she called Lord. In essence, each was saying, "I am changed; I am finding hope and meaning, and God did it." Before the closing session, Chuck and I slipped away to Washington, D.C. We had been invited to President Nixon's annual congressional prayer breakfast. Our friends had raised the necessary money for Beth Ann, Chuck, and me to attend.

We arrived in Washington in the midst of freezing weather, however, this did not dampen our spirits. We were too exhilarated with the promise of tomorrow, and the next day proved to be a full one. We started with the prayer breakfast itself. With so many secret service men around, we found it difficult to act normally. Chuck's camera was immediately confiscated. When we walked inside, we saw more than a thousand people. On hearing that the president's cabinet, most of the congressmen, and many executive heads from all over the land were in attendance, besides the president himself, we better understood the need for such extreme caution. We were impressed with the quality of the speeches. After the breakfast, Chuck attended the clergy seminar, and I attended a coffee given by the senators' wives. I was surprised to hear that these wives often met for prayer and fellowship. At lunch, Billy Graham gave the keynote address, and then we attended the final clergy seminar together.

I hated to see such an exciting day come to an end, for besides the activities we made two new friends, a Presbyterian minister and his wife. Ed and Olyva lived in a small town on the outskirts of Pittsburgh, Pennsylvania. As we were telling them good-by, Olyva threw her arms around me, gave me a big hug, and said, "Before I came here, I prayed that God would lead me to whomever he wanted me to meet; I am convinced that you and Chuck are the couple." I hugged Olyva back but didn't put much credence in her remark. After all, she lived way up close to Pittsburgh, Pennsylvania and I lived way down in Austin, Texas. It would be unlikely that our paths would ever cross again.

We stayed two more days to tour D.C. and then flew home. After the usual ceremony of welcoming hugs and kisses from Heather and Laura, and after showing them the treasures we had brought, we began to read our backlog of mail. I came across a letter from the Pittsburgh Experiment. Thinking it was probably just another plea for monetary assistance, I casually delegated it to a lesser station and read the "important" mail first. When we finally opened the letter, we discovered it was a possible job offer. Unsuccessfully, the Pittsburgh Experiment had been looking for someone to take Don James's place. Don, an Episcopal priest and former director of the Experiment, had died two years ago; Paul Everett, a Presbyterian minister, had succeeded Don as director. They were searching for an associate. Ever since Sam Shoemaker began the Experiment, an Episcopal priest had been connected with it. The leaders wanted to continue this policy, but after two years of searching, they had not found the right man. Evangelical Episcopal priests seemed to be as rare as perfect sand dollars on Texas beaches. When they heard of Chuck, his background in business plus his conversion under Sam Shoemaker, they became excited. Chuck sounded like the man they were seeking! On the same Sunday that Paul Everett flew down to interview Chuck, the calling committee of a large church in Oklahoma also flew down for an interview. For many months they had been looking for a new rector; they thought Chuck just might be the man.

Several days later Paul Everett called from Pittsburgh: "Would you and Carolyn please fly up here and let us show you this situation so that I can get some sleep?" Paul had reported to the board that Chuck seemed right for the job even though he wasn't a "flashy" leader. He had described Chuck as "more like a steady harbor in the midst of a storm." In unison the board said, "Paul, we have all been praying for a steady harbor. Get him to come!" Chuck told Paul that his heart was really in the parish ministry and that he had no real desire to leave it. He told him that Paul would probably be wasting his money to fly us up there. Paul replied, "Chuck, come on; this is God's money and his business. Many people up here have been praying about this choice. We feel that you're our man." Chuck set a date in March for our visit. He then received a phone call from the senior warden of the church in Oklahoma. The warden wanted us to fly to Oklahoma and consider their situation. Chuck set another date in March. He was off rattling God's doorknobs again!

In a month's time we were to make two trips! Almost nine months had passed since that Laity Lodge departure when Chuck had first startled me with his announcement. He had even been allowed to stay and participate in the Venture of Faith. I felt an anxious gnawing around my heart. One of these calls might herald new ministry and adventure for Chuck and me. Both were outside of Texas, and I had never lived anywhere else. Oklahoma was close by, but what if Chuck felt God calling him to Pittsburgh? I had only been in Pittsburgh once before; that was a visit in March 1954. I remember viewing the old city with stark disbelief. How could any place in the United States of America be so ugly, so bleak, so black with the grime of coal dust, so void of light and life? I could not even imagine God wanting to walk in his own story in sooty Pittsburgh!

As the time for our two trips grew near, I became more anxious. Frequently, I would set about amassing all of the possible problems one might encounter living in each place; then I would set about solving each one. Our friends, Ross and Ronnie, sensitive to my emotional state, invited me to go with them to a retreat at Beachhead in Port Aransas, Texas. Chuck encouraged me to go, so I accepted. As I walked down the path to the first session of the retreat, I was aware that the Texas wind was raw and blustery. It matched the state of my soul; I was impatient with God and man, weary of the waiting game. Very much the center of my own life, I was anxious for something to happen, yet I was just as anxious because something might happen.

I walked into the meeting room and took a back seat; normally, I am up front to be assured of not missing a word. But this day, I was in no hurry to hear any of the words. I really preferred to sit on the back row and sulk in my misery. The leader said that he was going to open the meeting by reading a Scripture. We were to listen and then spend the next thirty minutes outside in silence, reflecting on the Scripture.

Most people chose to walk along the beach. I took three steps and sat down in the nearest chair. After a few pouting minutes, I pulled out my thoughts and looked at them. Then I wrote:

Lord, I am not with these people; I am not hearing or even wanting to hear their sounds; I am in need of you. I am always in need of you, but sometimes I allow you to reach me more than at other times.

The man at the pool at Bethsaida was facing a change; I am facing a change; I trust you most of the time; I have peace most of the time; I have joyful expectation most of the time, but the time that slips through without my awareness of you can be filled with fears, fears of all kinds —

Fears of not succeeding, fears of succeeding, for either without you as the core, the anchor of my life would be disastrous. Fear of rejection, lostness, fear of acceptance, and thus possible neglect of the precious ones you have given me to care for. Fear of the weather, the cold of the wind, the cold of the people; fear of missing my husband whom I love and like, fear of losing my identity, or perhaps fear of having to take on a new identity, a new garb, garment of not my own choosing; fear of giving up more of me to more of you and yours. All fears, all real, yet in the moments in between, in the times that I can feel your hand upon mine, your touch, gentle, yet firm upon my heart, your guidance, your peace, I know as I know that the sun is there, and the moon is there, and the earth is to stand on, that I can and must do all things through you who strengthens me, that nothing can really separate me from you and your love; that in risking I find the wealth, the true wealth and meaning of life, the true value, quality of walking this world's path; that now that I have tasted this vintage of wine, surely all other drink would taste sour in comparison.

I have set, no, you have set my feet on this way, and though I shall stumble, stop, sit down, lag, sometimes even rush ahead too fast, there is no other way now that will fill my mold, the mold within my heart, your mold.

Give me your strength and your love to call upon, to claim, and help me to be your obedient one in the soon-to-be new chapter in my life.

Let me have eyes to see, and ears to hear, and a tongue to keep praising you and pointing to you and giving you the glory.

Our time was up; the leader was calling us back inside. Although the wind was still as raw and blustery as ever, I felt a new warm breeze blowing within my soul, and for a while I was all right. I went inside, and this time I sat on the front row to hear my friend, Dr. Myron Madden, speak about Significant Loss. I felt that soon I might be experiencing significant loss in my own life.

10

Three Rivers

Airports always sing of excitement, and in the past, for me, flying had always signalled a special journey. On this particular morning in March I was excited, but I was also apprehensive — not about the ability of the pilot or the crew to keep the plane in flight until we reached our destination, but about the destination itself. Chuck and I were enroute to Pittsburgh! If we were honest, we each hoped to find a locked door when we rattled this doorknob.

Although he thought it was time to leave St. David's Church, Chuck had no desire to leave the parish ministry. He saw himself as pastor of a local congregation. Many of today's priests have left parish life, declaring the institutional church to be a hopeless arena for life and ministry. Chuck, however, still had great hopes and vision and a deep belief in the parish church and her people. Even seeing all of her defects and problems, he felt that this was where his ministry was to be lived out. In class one day, John Knox had said, "If the church remembers who she is, you can be sure she will remember what she is supposed to do," and that applied to the institutional church too. Chuck just assumed that his next call would be as rector of an Episcopal church.

My reason for apprehension was simple: Pittsburgh was too far away from home and loved ones. Too, I still remembered how dirty and smudged her face was. Who would ever choose to live in Pittsburgh? Certainly not I! So we were silent for much of the long flight, each of us spinning his own "what if" dramas. In our better moments we had each said, "Lord, we really do want to walk with you in your story; help us to discern the way."

When we left Texas, it was warm and sunny, spring evidences everywhere. When we arrived in Pittsburgh, it was overcast and very cold: winter still had her austere cloak spread over the land. I don't recall seeing the sun at all during our visit. Paul Everett met us at the airport. Paul has such joy in his heart and such zest for life that with his entry even winter began to lose some of her severity.

Driving into the city, I was surprised to see that someone had washed Pittsburgh's face! Local residents tell the legend that Mrs. Mellon told Mr. Mellon, "If you want me to live in that dirty old city, you will just have to clean her up." And he did, or someone did. Many of the grimy, black buildings that I remembered so well had all been sandblasted. A beautiful park had been built in the middle of the city. As Paul pointed out the spot where the Monongahela and the Allegheny Rivers flow together to mark the beginning of the great Ohio River, I sensed the current of history flowing in those old river beds. George Washington himself, as a young engineer, had selected the site for the fort. Any early pioneers choosing to travel west most likely went down the Ohio River. If I were apprehensive over a change, how much more so must have been those brave souls who dared to risk, even at the loss of a precious homeland? I was caught up in an intense feeling of history and history begetters as we drove by the three rivers.

Pittsburgh herself was an old, old lady who had seen much life and living; however, unlike most old ladies, I sensed that her heartbeat was rapid, her vision unlimited, and her health thriving! The mining section spread out before us, smokestacks silhouetted against the sky. Three Rivers Stadium was a study in contrasts when viewed against the smokestacks and antiquated buildings. How Pittsburgh loves her baseball and her Pirates! But she is also a city of churches. Over a hundred ethnic groups live in Pittsburgh; so the churches take many shapes, both in nature and in construction. Roman Catholic and Presbyterian churches are the most numerous. As Paul drove into the suburbs, I was surprised to see that Pittsburgh is really a bundle of many hills laced together by rivers and streams, and I was amazed at the sheer beauty. At every turn I was presented with another "Grandma Moses" landscape. Much of Pittsburgh might be old and bleak and smoggy, but she possessed a vibrant, dancing splendor.

Paul drove into his driveway, and his two small children, Jeniffer and Christopher, came tumbling out to greet us. Then we met lovely, blond Maggie, Paul's wife and the daughter of Norman Vincent Peale. There is a special genuineness about Maggie; instantly, I sensed a new friendship in the making.

After dinner many of the Pittsburgh Experiment trustees arrived. Paul said, "So that the Huffmans can get to know us better, let's go around the room and each share who we are and how God became real to us." Their stories began. Had I closed my eyes, I could have easily imagined myself back home in Texas, listening to similar stories from similar groups. The God who was doing business with us Texans was also doing business with these Pennsylvanians! The same Holy Spirit had been active in the lives of these strangers! I called them strangers, but I remembered that someone had once said that all of us Christians had met a long, long time ago at the foot of the cross. In essence the stories were the same: "This is the way I was; God entered my life in a real way; now I am different, I am changed, and God did it." There was a banker, florist, advertising man, artist, stockbroker, realtor, lawyer, and so on. Many walks of life were represented. One big Irishman said, "I was a con man before I met the Lord Jesus Christ." One young man thanked God for his many, many blessings; those in the room knew that his wife was a brittle diabetic who had been a critical invalid for close to twenty years. On and on the stories continued. Then Chuck shared his story. Later in the meeting he prayed that he would discern God's will for his life and that he would then have the courage to do it. The room was charged with emotion. Regardless of the future, we would all remember this evening. As we said goodnight to return to the hotel, snowflakes had begun to fall — just another touch of magic to God's story. That night before crawling into bed, we took one last look from our hotel window. We had a postcard view of the three rivers and the city. As Chuck and I looked out, we both began to feel that Pittsburgh might not be so easily erased from our life's plan.

The next morning we breakfasted with other trustees of the Experiment. Although these were different Christians from the ones we had met before, they too were trying to be God's persons in the midst of living out their lives. All were aware of our pending Oklahoma trip. After breakfast one man hugged me and said, "I don't know what God has in store for you two, but he surely does have his hand on your shoulders. I hope I'm around to see what happens."

That afternoon we went to the Hill District and met another trustee, Tom O'Brien. Tom was in charge of St. Joseph's House of Hospitality. The Hill is known to be one of the worst slum areas in America. Tom, a wiry little Irishman, was running in God's story; walking was too slow! Fifteen years ago, before his conversion to Christianity, Tom encountered his old drinking buddy, Don James. Since Don was attired in a priest's garb, Tom's greeting was, "What masquerade party are you going to?" Unknown to Tom, Don had discovered the God who wants to do business with his people. He had become an Episcopal priest and was director of the Pittsburgh Experiment. Don was changed, and God in Christ had done it. Tom became involved with Don and the fellowship groups, and he too became a changed man because of Jesus Christ.

Now Tom was helping other lost men, the rejects of society, to find a place. He would love them, house them, feed them, clothe them, and even give them aptitude tests to help them discover their hidden potential. Tom supported them while they were being trained for a trade. How they loved him! He did not drown them with his own Christian beliefs, but whenever the question of the source of Tom's own strength would arise, he was always ready to speak about the reality and power of God in his life. Redemption of broken lives was being enacted over and over again in this old house on the Hill. Tom would not call what he was doing social action; he chose to call it *applied Christian action.* He said that in his own strength he would have run out of steam long ago, but because Jesus Christ was in him, and because he was trying to do this for him, he found lasting, sustaining power. As we left the Hill, Paul remarked, "I have heard it said that if you want anything good done in this city just ask Tom O'Brien. Some call him the most influential man in Pittsburgh." I could well believe it.

Our next stop was at a halfway house for men in the process of being released from prison. Sam Shoemaker once said that Christians needed to "get changed, get together, get going." Well, Dwight Koerber, a lawyer, got changed through Jesus Christ, got together with other Christian men in the Pittsburgh Experiment, and then got the vision that he needed to get going. He felt a particular concern for the men in prison. Dwight knew that the return rate to prison is about 85 percent. Most who are discharged are either the same men or worse than when they first entered prison.

Dwight dreamed a dream and grasped the vision of a Christian group being started inside prison walls. He felt that if the men could encounter the same Christ he had encountered then they would be new creatures with a bright chance of changing the discouraging return statistics. Dwight met opposition and encountered red tape, but he kept working toward his dream. After several years, he and some others were

allowed to start a Christian group inside the maximum security prison. They called the group Alpha. Then they started a
second group in a halfway house. Any man who wanted to
attend was welcome. Then a third group started, a fellowship
outside in the community. Its purpose was to continue to
support a man after he was paroled. This group was made up of
offenders who could say, "I know how you feel, for I have been
there," and of Pittsburgh Experiment men who, though they
had never been in prison, could still say, "We care for you and
are here to try and reach out when you need us." They all could
say, "Has anybody told you today that God loves you?"

Since this program began, only two men who have participated in the prayer fellowship groups have ever returned to
prison. Dwight's dream has paid off. Later they showed us a
place in downtown Pittsburgh called the Pittsburgh Power and
Light Company, an exciting new ministry of the Experiment's.
It was led by Bob Letsinger, a young Presbyterian minister. Its
outreach was the many, many college-age students in the city.
Christians who worked there served a delicious lunchtime
"power burger"; they were also ready to reach out to anyone
who was hurting.

As we left, my head was spinning with the life and vitality I
had seen churning all around us. Evidently many people had
taken Sam Shoemaker seriously when he threw down the
challenge, "Let's make Pittsburgh as well known for God as it
is for steel." They were on their way!

We felt we could not leave Pittsburgh without visiting old
Calvary Episcopal Church. At first glimpse, I was surprised. I
was not prepared for such a magnificent edifice. Calvary
looked like a cathedral. We stepped inside. It was impossible to
absorb the fullness of the beauty — stained-glass windows,
elegant interior, indescribable hand-carved chancel area. "This
was Sam Shoemaker's church," I thought. Then I corrected
myself: "No, this is God's church, only *used* by Sam
Shoemaker." The large hand-carved mahogany pulpit was

impressive. I could easily picture Sam standing there enthusiastically urging, "Christians, come all the way in where
the fun is!" For a few minutes, Chuck stood in the pulpit; then
we left. Who would have told us about the Holy Spirit had not
Sam entered our lives?

That evening we were taken to a very exclusive restaurant
on the top of Mt. Washington. It hung over the very edge of the
mountain. Besides the food being excellent, it was known for
its outstanding view of the city. We arrived at dusk just in time
to watch the metamorphosis take place. One by one, thousands
of lights came on all over the city. As it became dark, the lights
were reflected in the rivers below. It was reminiscent of
mystical castle lands described in long-ago fairy tales. One of
the trustees said, "Chuck, this is your parish. I give you the
city of Pittsburgh." Chuck looked like he might like to deal
with this kind of challenge. But I thought, "Shepherd to so
many sheep in such a faraway cold land?" Then I comforted
myself with the thought of the pending Oklahoma trip. Chuck
really did love the parish ministry. Wasn't this Pittsburgh trip
just another exciting interval in our long adventure of walking
in God's story?

Paul took us to the airport the next morning. We told him
good-by and boarded the plane. As we headed home, we had
much to consider. Pittsburgh was quite a lady.

11

Oklahoma

Once again we were at the airport, and once again I was apprehensive. This time our destination was Oklahoma. And once again I prayed, "Lord, help us to see your will for our lives." Chuck had been so certain over his call to the ministry. This time I hoped he would clearly hear the call heralding his next assignment. We were in flight, and except for the hum of the motors, things were silent. I was shuffling my "what if" deck again. Chuck must have been doing the same. Secretly I held great expectations for this trip. I hoped that we would discover this Oklahoma church to be custom built for Chuck Huffman. I anticipated instant love between Chuck and the big old church, with the promise of a great "marriage" between the two. After seeing how far Pittsburgh was from Texas, Oklahoma seemed a stone's throw away. My hopes were riding high.

When we landed, we were met by the chairman of the calling committee, a fine doctor whom we had met before. I remember that he kept asking me about Chuck's health and the longevity of his ancestors. It had been a year since the last rector had died, and this doctor had spent much time and concern in searching for a new rector. He hoped to get a healthy man who would stay around for a long time. He even told Chuck that if he became rector of that parish he would enroll him in a twice-a-week exercise program at the Y. If

Chuck chose to come here, I could feel confident that someone besides myself would be riding herd on his health. The doctor left us at the hotel, promising to see us the next day.

Enroute to tour the church the following morning, my mind raced: What would she look like? Would we feel a part of her bloodstream? The church turned out to be a large old stone building, very traditional, very impressive. The sanctuary itself was beautiful with many stained-glass windows, and the pulpit was massive — tall and built of solid, grey marble. In my mind's eye, I visualized Chuck standing in that immense pulpit, but the picture seemed blurry. Next we saw the rector's office; it seemed more like a museum than an office. It was very large with its own adjoining private chapel, and the antique furniture was priceless. The desk itself was one of the largest, most beautiful mahogany pieces I had ever seen. On the walls were icons, old paintings, and various wall hangings, some dating back to the sixteenth and seventeenth centuries. I felt as if it would be almost improper to speak above a whisper in that still, dark room.

That night was important, for Chuck was to speak to the vestry. He was anxious to present a true picture of himself. As far as he was able, he wanted to tear off the "brown wrapping paper" and reveal exactly who he was and what he really believed. He wanted them to know what was important to him. Wouldn't it be terrible for the men to purchase one package only to discover on opening it "Christmas morning" that they had really been given something else? He and the doctor left around 7:00, and it was midnight before they returned. The doctor came over to me and said, "Well, you should have seen your husband tonight; he was inspired! I don't know what he is going to do, but I can tell you this: he has his feet on the ground and knows what he is about. I wish him Godspeed."

We returned to the hotel, and Chuck began to tell me about the meeting. He said he began by telling his own story. He told of Carl, of his own encounter with God, and of his becoming a priest. He spoke of the God who wants to be involved with his people through the power of his Holy Spirit. Then he told them about the Pittsburgh Experiment. He spoke of lives being changed and brokenness being mended through men meeting together in Christian fellowship. His was an evangelical approach, and he wanted these men to know it. They had all seemed to listen intently. After the meeting, a young man approached Chuck and softly whispered, "Chuck, will you pray for me? I was fired two weeks ago and have no promise of another position."

Chuck agreed to pray for the man and then said, "Do any of these people know of your dilemma?"

"Oh, no!" said the young man, "I haven't shared this with any of them."

Chuck had seen similar situations repeated again and again. Men sit next to one another, say the proper words at the proper time, and play the game well; yet, unknown to all, a heart is exploding! Chuck was shown anew the benefits and blessings that can emerge from small groups of Christians willing to risk being vulnerable in the hope of reaching out and supporting some hurting heart. After promising again to pray for the young man, Chuck left the meeting.

It was late, and we turned out the lights. Sleep came quickly for Chuck, but for me it was nowhere in sight. My head was still spinning. These two days really had not gone at all according to my hidden agenda; where I had imagined Chuck's singing of a possible marriage between priest and parish in Oklahoma, he was still singing songs of the Pittsburgh Experiment!

After we finished packing the next morning, Chuck said he would continue to pray about both places. Whether he realized it or not, I felt he had already written in his logbook: "Oklahoma doorknob sufficiently rattled, but door refused to open." I was by myself, for Chuck had gone to check out of the hotel. Looking in the mirror as I combed my hair, I mused over all the priests who would be thrilled to be considered as rector of such a large, important church as this one. Unquestionably, it would be a great honor to claim this church as home base. I remembered the elegant, impressive vestments I had seen in the old church; they were there just waiting to be claimed by the new rector. Too, I could just imagine the lovely rectory that the parish would provide. In response to my thinking of leaving all this behind, I said, "See, Lord, we will even give up status for you." And the little voice that usually whispers so faintly inside one's inner being shouted, "Yes, but will you take on status for me?" The statement was so clear that I gasped out loud! And I knew that some day I might have to be willing to take on status for him.

Chuck said, "Let's go," and once more we were off to the airport. During the flight he was busy with paper and pencil. He was trying to be very realistic. With his analytical head, Chuck was attempting to list the pros and cons of both Pittsburgh and Oklahoma ministries. My head, in its usual fashion, was spinning thoughts so rapidly that I had to set them down to get rid of them:

Where to fly, dear Lord? How to know? Where to soar for you? To walk for you? To speak, to sing your praise? Which way? Can you, would you send a small portion of Heaven's wisdom down our way? Would you allay the turmoil, still the spinning storm of anxiety that is racing round my soul? We do trust you and want to be your people in the brokenness in the world all around us, but, O Lord, which way?

You have promised to go before and make the crooked way straight, to be there both in the dells of valleys and crests of hills, when the wind blows too cold, and when the dry seasons of the soul come. But where, O Lord, where do you lead?

Must I, must we, take the small, hesitant, unsteady, adventurous step out in the direction of our heart's own choosing, hoping it is your own choosing too? We have claimed truly to want to follow you wherever you direct, have prayed for your guidance. Will it only be in reflection, in looking back across the shadows and highlights of our walk that we can say, "Yes, surely, this was the way that he would have had us to go"? And, if we have erred in our direction in clearly hearing the still, small voice, can we but claim the promise that you will take our blundering errors, our misplaced steps, and use them also for your glory?

This I believe, must believe, and must hold fast to as we step out in faith with you, and for you, anticipating great joy and sustenance in the knowledge that you are truly always there, the Alpha and Omega of all time loving and caring for us.

When I read what I had written to Chuck, he tossed aside his list. He was remembering an offer: "Chuck, this is your parish. I give you the city of Pittsburgh!" What an opportunity! What a challenge! What a privilege to follow in the steps of Sam Shoemaker! It almost seemed as if the script had been written with Chuck Huffman in mind!

When we reached home that night, Chuck told the girls that it looked as if all roads were leading to Pittsburgh. The girls' first response was, "But, daddy, we can't go there. They don't have any Mexican food!" My children might be worrying about Mexican food, but I had just donned the coat of cold, stark reality! It looked as if I were really going to move to Pittsburgh. Had the Lord forgotten how cold natured I was? It was easy to sit in a warm living room in the midst of Christian fellowship and pray, "Lord, I want to walk with you in your story. I want to be your instrument, use me." But this was carrying things just a little too far! It looked as if I was getting in that rickety old wheelbarrow again, but this time the wire seemed half as wide and twice as high. Being a Christian is risky business.

12

Praise the Lord Anyhow

Obedience

I said, "Let me walk in the field,"
He said, "No, walk in the town."
I said, "There are no flowers there."
He said, "No flowers but a crown."

I said, "But the skies are black,
There is nothing but noise and din."
And He wept as He sent me back;
"There is more," He said, "there is sin."

I said, "But the air is thick
And fogs are veiling the sun."
He answered, "Yet souls are sick,
And souls in the dark undone."

I said, "I shall miss the light
And friends will miss me, they say."
He answered, "Choose tonight
If I am to miss you, or they."

I pleaded for time to be given,
He said, "Is it hard to decide?
It will not seem hard in Heaven
To have followed the steps of your Guide."

I cast one look at the fields,
Then set my face to the town;
He said, "My child, do you yield?
Will you leave the flowers for the crown?"

Then into His hand went mine;
And into my heart came He;
And I walk in a light divine,
The path I had feared to see.[1]

While in seminary, I had discovered this peom written by
George MacDonald. It was meaningful to me then, and as I
reread the words, they became even more significant. The
lines, "But the skies are black, there is nothing but noise and
din," and "But the air is thick and fogs are veiling the sun"
described only one place — Pittsburgh! "I shall miss the light,"
held a double meaning. I would surely miss the spiritual light
that I had been receiving from so many people in Texas, and I
would also miss the light of the beautiful bright Texas sky.
Until seen in contrast with other places, I had taken for
granted this clear coverlet of blue. Barbara, a young girl from
Pennsylvania, visited Texas for the first time. She looked up
into the sky and said in amazement, "Oh, daddy, everything
seems so bright and blue here!"

I would miss the startling brightness of a Texas sky and her
lovely sunsets, but I knew I had no choice. I really did have to
yield and leave the flowers, those beautiful Texas bluebonnets,
for the crown. Like Chuck, I felt that God had business for us in
Pittsburgh. "After all," I thought, "after surviving the death of
one small boy, surely I can easily handle a Pittsburgh!"

In April we flew back to Pennsylvania to buy a house. We
knew that we would not actually move until July, but it was
important for me to have a "nest" there waiting. Pittsburgh
was still cold and covered with winter. The only promises of
spring were the bright yellow forsythia bushes. How lovely
they were!

After three days of diligent searching, we bought a typical
two-story salt-box. Although we had been warned that the cost
of living in Pittsburgh would be considerably higher than back
home, we were still shocked at prices. Since there had been

only two children in our present neighborhood, I had prayed, "Lord, let us move into a neighborhood with children." I felt that if my girls had friends, it would make their adjustment much easier. Be careful in what you pray! My salt-box stood at the end of one short block in North Hills. There were thirty children on the one small street! ("Lord, I really had a much smaller number in mind!") The view from my kitchen window was breathtaking. It was another Grandma Moses landscape. Choosing our carpet color, we became very bold. Why not ruby red! Then when the days were particularly gray and dreary, our bright red floors would add a cheerful note.

During the house-buying trip, there was only one time when we both panicked. We had been sent by the realty company to secure our mortgage. They had loaned us a car and had carefully given us directions to get to a mortgage company that was located in Bellevue. On arrival, we discovered Bellevue to be an old, old small borough in Pennsylvania. Very little of anything was stirring. As we moved through the doors of the First Federal Savings building, Chuck and I both stopped still in our tracks. It was as if we were puppets who had suddenly lost our puppeteer! It was as if we had been walking in a dream world only to step back through the hole of reality. We both looked at each other and said, "Just what in the world are we doing in this little old borough preparing to buy a house? What are we doing investing our equity in Pennsylvania soil? What kind of craziness is this Christian business anyway?" Then, I guess, as George MacDonald's last verse states:

> Into His hand went mine,
> And into my heart came He
> And I walk in a light divine,
> The path I had feared to see.[2]

We were all right once again. We were still in the land of reality, but this time we were walking in God's reality and in his story.

At the airport we visted briefly with Ed and Olyva, our new friends from the presidential prayer breakfast. We had written them of our new assignment. Olyva's earlier words now took on deeper meaning. We flew home to begin the massive task of transplanting five Texans, two dogs, and one calico cat to Pittsburgh, Pennsylvania.

The next three and one-half months were a patchwork quilt of emotions. Woven into the pattern were tears, anticipation, joy, and just plain hard work. Yet throughout the coverlet ran the strong linen fiber of certainty that we were doing the right thing.

So many small vignettes were played out. I remember for example that Texas had been in the middle of a drouth; for six months we had seen no rain in Austin. One day while I was at a drugstore, I noticed the sign, "Sale on all umbrellas — half price." Recalling what I had observed and heard about Pittsburgh and her rainy weather, I decided to take advantage of the sale. After selecting three bright umbrellas, I stood in line to be checked out. I noticed one man staring at me. Finally, he walked over and said, "Lady, I can't stand it any longer. Do you know something that I don't know?" It was a clear day with no cloud in sight. Laughing, I told him I was moving to Pittsburgh, Pennsylvania, and felt that I might have need of many umbrellas. On hearing of my destination, the man suggested I buy several more. He had once lived in Pittsburgh!

Much of my time before the move was spent getting our beautiful white house presentable. She had to be cleaned and polished before we could put the For Sale sign out front. One morning in May, Mary Allen and Alice Jean arrived with bucket in one hand and Spic and Span in the other. They had even brought their own tea to drink. "We've come to help you clean your woodwork!" These were close friends; we had been together in a small in-depth Bible study group. It was one thing to share the gospel with them, but I hated to share my dirty woodwork. They were both such good housekeepers! It was a known fact that I would much rather pray than scrub any day. But, they were here, and the distasteful task needed doing, so off we started. That night I was bone weary as I reflected on my day.

> Dear Lord, I do *not* enjoy being "Martha." Truly, you were right in saying that Mary had chosen the better way. Getting a house ready for a new owner is not an easy task! I would much rather sit at your feet than sit at the bottom of a flight of stairs in dire need of scrubbing!
>
> In part, this calls to mind your getting me ready for a new nature, your nature. Just as I cannot instantly create a new spotless dwelling, I must remind myself that you do not plan instantly to create a new me! There have to be cobwebs to ferret out, dust to wipe away, black marks to erase, and window panes to shine to a glistening brightness.
>
> Yet, just as I know that there are nooks and crannies in this big, white house of mine that shall never be truly dust free, so I know that there are places in this finite dwelling, this being of mine that shall never be "truly dust free" until they pass through the final filter of your love.
>
> Thank you for loving me as I am even though the dust continues to blow and the dirty debris seems to accumulate and even find its way back into the domain of my soul.

In less than three weeks my lovely old house was sold; so I was free to concentrate on other things. We were all having physical examinations before starting out into the unknown frontierland. Beth Ann had gone in for her checkup. The doctor called to tell me that he wanted Beth Ann to come back to his office for some more tests and x-rays. He suspected that she might have the beginning of rheumatoid arthritis. "Don't worry," he said, "I just want to check her out." Telling me not to worry about my children's health was like telling me not to breathe. Except for concern over the health of my girls (and Chuck), I have been fairly successful in eventually relinquishing problems and bearded situations to God (though I often seem to yank them back). Chuck sometimes wonders about my ability to erase worry from my blackboard of thought. But because of what happened so quickly to Carl, I am a wobbly piece of spaghetti in the face of any possible illness of my girls. I have to fall on my knees and demand help from the Heavenly Father! So confronting the doctor's suspicion about Beth Ann, I went swimming again in the basin of fear and trembling. My other apprehensions and concerns about our move seemed to polarize in this one raw spot! What had I heard about rheumatoid arthritis? Wasn't it very painful? Wasn't the worst possible environment a cold, damp winterland like Pittsburgh? Lord, what are you thinking of?

> Don't you know I get tired, weary, spent, drained, lost in walking through this life with you, Lord? Don't you know I love so hard, give so much, reach out so far, become so immersed in this business of caring that I become engulfed in the pure passion of it? In the pattern of hurting so? It hurts to love. It would be so much safer to learn to live behind the wall of feelings, to avoid the mesh of vulnerability, but just how does one stop loving?
>
> How does one discontinue loving a son, a daughter, a husband, a mother, a father, a brother, a sister, a friend — a God? There are days when I wish I knew, for then I would escape the pain that comes with loving, and I would disappear silently on to the path of no hurt, no pain, no compassion, no involvement, no love, and thus no life!
>
> Why did you plan the plan this way? Your plan, Lord, your scheme of life? Oh, I know that you answered Job, but that does not stifle my same, seeking question of "Why, why, Lord?" A question that will never see an answer in this world, a question that I rarely ask, but I am tired of hurting, and I need to cry out tonight, *"Why?"*

> I know that you love me and mine. I know that you hold us in the palm of your hand. I know that you are always there, but I am still tired tonight, and still hurting tonight, and still fearing tonight. You seem to have escaped into the shadows; yet, in reality, I really perceive that it is I who have pulled down the dark shadows over and around me.

Perhaps tonight I shall rest, and tomorrow I can say, "This is the day that the Lord hath made," and allow you to work in my being again, and feel your power, and your reality in this small, finite life of mine. Touch me!

The next morning Ernestlea called. We had known each other a long time. We had been agnostics together in Houston, and now we were trying to follow the same Lord in Austin. This particular morning, she was in a valley mood. There had been many small aggravating crises with each member of her family, and Ernestlea was tired and angry with the whole world. She admitted being frustrated with the roles of wife, mother, daughter, friend — disciple. There was a short pause, then she said, "I'm ashamed to share such black thoughts with you, Carolyn. You're such a good Christian that you would *never* think this way."

"Wait a minute," I said, "I have something to share with you; I wrote it only last night." I returned to the phone and started reading, "Don't you know I get tired, weary, spent, drained, lost in walking through this life with you, Lord?"

When I finished, there was silence; then softly Ernestlea said, "That is the greatest gift you could have given to me. I did not know that you had any such cracks in your Christian life. I will be over in fifteen minutes to get a copy." The power of the personal again! Several days later I received the good news from the doctor: "Beth Ann is just fine!"

Daily in an attempt to dimish our material possessions, I would go through closets and sort through drawers. I had to face it. We were all packrats! And each of us "rats" wanted to keep his own special hoarded cheese! It was a simple matter to suggest that Chuck's World War II parachute really should be discarded. It was not as simple to hear him suggest that my stack representing many years of collecting Christmas magazines, recipes, and "do it yourself" books was really unnecessary. We were not having much success in encouraging our three daughters to "cut to the bone" either. Each stuffed animal and old book was a priceless memento! I was able to be more firm with Heather and Laura than with Beth Ann. Heather and Laura were eagerly anticipating our new adventure. Already they were dreaming of sled rides and snowmen!

In contrast, Beth Ann looked upon the pending move as the end of life itself; her emotional boat, which was usually even keel, rocked with such upheaval that I hated to suggest she leave anything behind. One evening in June Beth Ann, upset with life and living, came into my room and cried and cried. Perhaps we could go to Pittsburgh and she could stay here, she suggested. She was leaving her friends, her white house with the spiral staircase, her beloved land, Texas. She had grief-work to do, and she was doing it. When I told her that we really could not leave without her, she sobbed harder. Nothing that I said seemed to comfort her, and the tears continued to flow. Storming into Chuck's study, I told him about Beth Ann's plight. I insisted that he call Paul Everett in Pittsburgh and remind him that he was going to have some Christian young people write Beth Ann a few "Welcome to Pittsburgh" letters!

Chuck tried to calm me down; then he gave me a five-point sermon on the redemptive nature of tears and the great value of lessons learned in working through the stresses and trials of life. No, he would *not* call Paul Everett! But he would go talk with Beth Ann. In a few minutes, fresh from Beth Ann's tears, Chuck returned. He said, "You know I do have some important business that I need to discuss with Paul. I'll call him tonight." Chuck went to make the phone call, and I went to talk to my Heavenly Father.

Here we are again, Lord, just you and I, inside my mind, my skin, seeing my frightened, frenzied thoughts spin around my head like a whirlwind of pain and fear. I try not to listen to these fragmented, anticipating, screaming, though silent, thoughts.

Lord, I tell myself that I trust you in this situation with this dear one. I turn Beth Ann back over to you again as I have done so many times in the past, knowing that you love her more than I do with my earthly love's limitation; knowing that you have things, all things, under your supreme authority; yet I still keep taking the pulse of my anticipatory, fraught fears and keep pulling this child back into my bundle of concerns.

Why do I do these things? *Why,* when I have felt such a reality of you in my life, do I forget so easily and begin to fear so swiftly? There is some solace in remembering Thomas's doubting, and Peter's denial, but I still feel discouragement when I consider my lack of trust in you who have been so good to me. There seems to be so much energy spent in worrying, energy that could be utilized for you. My lack of trust today has made my soul truly weary: "I believe, help my unbelief."

Lord, you say that it is in my weakness that your strength can be manifested. I do not ask to understand. I do ask that you take this weakness of mine tonight, this lack of trust, and in some way use it for your glory. Amen.

Beth Ann did receive some letters from Pittsburgh teen-agers, and her spirits lifted. She received a great letter of encouragement from Eleanor, the Pittsburgh Experiment secretary.

The weeks turned into months, and then the calendar really did say July. Our departure date was the last week in July. Things were closing in on me. We worked hard every day and attended farewell parties at night. And then came the final week itself. It was getting close to countdown time and blast off! We drove to San Antonio to tell my mother and dad good-by. How I dreaded being so far away from these dear ones. They had just finished reading Merlin Carothers' book, *Prison to Praise,* and they played his tape for us. Instead of saying, "In all things give thanks," he was suggesting, "For all things give thanks." This had worked in his own life. The next morning we kissed my parents and told them good-by. With tears streaming down their faces, they said, "Thank you, Lord, that our only daughter is moving so far away to Pittsburgh!" And, in some crazy unexplainable fashion, the leave-taking was wrapped in an affirmation of joy!

St. David's Church gave the Keith Millers and us a beautiful going-away party. Keith and Mary Allen were moving to Indiana for a year. Keith had contracted to teach at a seminary. As I considered the hundreds of friends around us who had come to wish us well, I saw afresh the bounty we were leaving behind.

Three days before departure, our calico cat had kittens. This was not on the agenda. The animals were being flown to Pittsburgh, so I had to call the movers and explain that the shipping crate would have to be enlarged — our feline family had just increased!

The night before our departure we told Lois and John Knox good-by! As I sat talking to this gentle man, I began to cry. My pent-up emotions and clustered sadness over leaving home began to flow. Tomorrow really was the day! We promised to correspond. Later John gave me a copy of his first book published in 1932. The jacket said, "A book of uncommon strength and beauty," and for me it proved to be just that. (I read it on the way to Pittsburgh.)

We left the Knoxes to spend the last night with Ernestlea and Paul Williams. The next morning we had breakfast, then started to gather our things. We were to meet Chuck's mother and dad, who were driving to Pittsburgh with us. Then we were to check our house and the big moving van one last time. As I hugged and kissed Paul and Ernestlea, I suddenly thought, *"We don't have a current will!* What if something should happen to us? No one would know who was to raise our children." Chuck and I had discussed these things but had not written them down. I pushed Ernestlea into her bedroom and sat down at her desk. "Give me some paper. I must write a fast will." Between tears and laughter, I wrote my "last will and testament" and handed it to Ernestlea. At first, I thought what an incongruous time to be thinking of wills and death. Then I reconsidered. Our leave-taking really did represent a death to an era in our life, so why not write a will? Between picture taking and hugs and kisses, we finally said good-by. On the back of our station wagon, you could see our brave new bumper sticker, Praise the Lord Anyhow!

"We are one in the Spirit, we are one in the Lord," or so goes the song. Regardless of the distance between Christian friends and loved ones, this is so. I know this is true. If my head knows this, then why is my heart breaking so? Why do I feel as if I have experienced something akin to open heart surgery? Why are leave-takings, good-bys, and the closing of chapters always so difficult? Why are we not allowed to put roots down too deeply in anything but you, Lord? Tearing up roots brings pain and cracks in emotions. Why did you ask us to "rejoice in all things," both the pleasures and the pain? This might be possible for a first-century Paul of Damascus, but it is very difficult for mother, wife, daughter, friend, flesh person, just trying to survive in this, your twentieth century.

Again, with my intellect, I have perceived that there is power and fulfillment in thanking you in adversity, and in praising you in pain, in relinquishing all things to your sovereignty. It is the heart that is so difficult to yoke. I sense that it is impossible for me to yoke this pulsating heart of mine. Only you can master it and give it the peace and joy that it truly seeks, and which are only yours to give.

If endings of chapters are difficult, then so are beginnings, but with you at the helm, surely I can manage both. I praise you and try to step out in mission for you — I *am* scared, though.

13

Sallying Forth

Shortly before our move, we had received a letter from Estelle Carver, saying, "I am storming the gates of heaven in behalf of the Huffmans and their move!" Well, the animals "reported" a great move, but ours turned out to be a comedy of errors. The van lines later told us that of two hundred fifty cross-country moves, our was by far the worst, and I believed them! The van load capacity was misjudged; so our earthly belongings came piecemeal. Moving from a large house into a smaller one also presented problems. Fitting our accumulation of furnishings into our brand-new salt-box took all of Chuck's engineering ingenuity. The first crisis arrived with the brightly painted wooden puppet theater which refused to squeeze through the basement door. Chuck located his saw, and began to remove the decorative molding on top. Stumbling under the weight of the theater, Chuck and one of the movers failed to shove it through the opening; it was still too tall. Again Chuck began to saw — this time from the bottom. As perspiration rolled down his face, he looked over at me and said, "If I didn't really think that God was in the midst of this whole move, I don't know that I could handle it." This time the assaulted theater fit through the door.

We have a massive library. Since there were limited bookcases in the Pittsburgh house, Chuck designed a beautiful bookcase unit and had it built in Austin. In order to utilize all the space, he had considered very carefully the dimensions of his study in Pittsburgh. The finished product was elegant. It consisted of two bases with doors, supporting an eight-foot long, green, formica desk top. On this top stood the third piece — the magnificent 8 by 5 foot bookcase unit itself. We were anxious to see this piece in Chuck's study. Two movers easily carried the two bases upstairs; then they carried in the formica desk top. But the bookcase unit would not clear the turn on the stairs! The movers merely backed down the stairs, carried the bookcase outside, and set it down in the front yard, with the words, "It will never make it," tossed lightly over their shoulders.

It began to thunder; storm clouds gathered. Rain threatened. And there sat our beautiful new bookcase naked in the front yard! Chuck suggested a plan to the men; they implemented it and safely carried the piece upstairs, but they were confused concerning just how the unit fit together. When I reached the point in my instructions where I said, "Then the bookcase sits on top of the formica top," they looked at me in disbelief.

The driver said firmly, "Lady, there is *no way* that *that* bookcase will sit on top of *that* desk top. It is just too tall. The ceiling is too low. *It will never make it.* Never!"

Before Chuck could say anything, I stood very tall (all five feet four inches of me) and declared, "Listen, before my husband was a priest, he was an engineer, and he designed this whole thing."

With those words still clinging to the air, the mover said through clenched teeth, "Lady, all I can say is it's a good thing he got out of engineering!" Poor Chuck, as if the day had not been traumatic enough, there he stood with his full ego on the chopping block! What if the bookcase *wouldn't* clear the ceiling? I am sure Chuck wished I would go wash my mouth out with soap and quit talking. The moment of truth arrived — up, up, up went the heavy, massive bookcase. It cleared the ceiling by two inches! In silence, the movers marched downstairs.

After unloading the truck, the driver said, "I'm sorry, but we are due in North Carolina. There is no way we can unpack you." They departed. Later the next afternoon, however, the van line sent out some very able helpers. Space will not allow me to mention all of the broken, lost, marred, scarred, chipped, and crushed items we discovered as we began the mammoth task of unpacking. Without Chuck's mother and dad to give us both moral and physical support, I wonder if we could have made it.

Chuck first unpacked our large oil painting, a Klee landscape that was very special to us. As he pulled it from the carton, he gasped, "Oh, no." Not only had the packers failed to wrap it, but someone had carelessly tossed an old antique picture inside the carton with it. This picture had rusty nails on the back which had badly scratched, marred, and penetrated the canvas. We discovered our sterling silverware tossed helter skelter in a box. No attempt had been made to wrap it. Laddie, Chuck's mother, shouted from the basement. She had discovered a can of East Texas molasses syrup tossed inside a carton with many other things. The lid had not been secured, and we found thick molasses dribbling down everything in the box!

Since we were rapidly running out of storage space, the solution had become, "Down to the basement!" We had no shelves down there yet, so Laddie and I decided to improvise. We took the sturdy empty cardboard boxes and stacked them on top of one another to produce — shelves. Pots and pans, old bric-a-brac, anything small enough to fit inside was placed on our pseudo shelves. Ben, Chuck's dad and a master craftsman, looked askance at our creative jungle gym. He did not think it looked very trustworthy. We felt however that it was doing its job well for the moment, and we had too much to do to worry about the future. We ignored his warning.

The next day I decided to do some laundry. My washing machine sounded strange and clattery, but I decided to ignore that too. As I left the basement, I observed the soap swishing through the clothes, and I thought, clattery or not, that old machine was doing the job it was cut out to do. Where one moment I knew stillness, the next I heard crashing, clanging, shattering, thumping, bumping, dumping — the washer had overflowed, soaking the bottoms of our cardboard "shelves." As each carton became sufficiently soaked, it collapsed bringing down with it the next layer and then the next. Before us lay a mess of swirling water, floating debris, soggy cardboard, and broken pieces of glass. Our beautiful shelves had been "killed." I discovered later that my washer and dryer had also been "killed" in the move. Bless Ben's heart, he never said one word of "I told you so" concerning the shelves. I crawled into bed that night too tired for tears.

Because of complex circumstances, we had no refrigerator for three weeks. With no refrigerator, no washer, no dryer, no vacuum cleaner (it was broken also), no T.V. (broken), and no lovely basement shelves, and most of all, no homeland, I found life difficult to juggle. Heralding our arrival, Maggie and Paul Everett had decorated our front door with a long WELCOME HUFFMANS banner. Bright crepe paper streamers hung all about. The welcome message had started out looking so cheerful; now, the writing was faded, and the streamers were limp and scraggly from the rain. In order to reach the bedraggled remains, I tiptoed to yank down the last remnant. I identified with these worn-out flags of welcome. I too had lost my "starch" and felt as limp, tired, and scraggly as they looked. I was homesick! Why hadn't someone warned me of the emotional upheaval involved in moving?

Lord, how far can you stretch a heart? I left so many pieces behind; so many dear ones' own fragments of this self-same squeezed-out heart that I feel I am living with a void, a yawning hole where once a heart dwelled. Ones who have you as the common denominator of their lives seem to hold such a special meaning for one another. It tears out roots to leave.

Will you fill the gaping hole that was once my heart so that I may allow your love to flow through to others, your people, in this new land that I shall be claiming as home? Surely you and only you can fill this emptiness that I feel. I alone have nothing to give, but I know if I only trust in you that you will see that your stream of living water and life continues to flow out and out.

Regardless of water in the basement, molasses in the box, and the absence of a refrigerator, I still had important, necessary tasks to do. Chuck made his daily sally into the city, leaving me to cope with some of the basic rudiments of living. Just finding my way around in this unknown land was a challenge. Back home, I was known as the girl who could get lost going from her kitchen to the garbage can. How could I possibly manage in this maze of Pittsburgh streets and hills? But there were things that could no longer be neglected. My girls had to be registered in schools, groceries had to be bought, and a beauty parlor had to be discovered. I have found that I can storm almost any citadel if my hair is properly set!

Another agenda item was getting our Pennsylvania driver's licenses. We had already been warned that this was no small accomplishment. Chuck and I studied our driver's manual and made our pilgrimage to a small town on the outskirts of the city. Many people were in the waiting room; so we sat down to wait our turn. When our names were called, we went in together. With the entrance of Chuck in his clerical collar, the policeman jumped to his feet and began to treat him like royalty. When he discovered that we were from Texas, he told us of his recent heart surgery in Houston. We discussed his health. Thinking of the many waiting people, I began to get nervous and finally mentioned the tests. He asked, "Did you study your manuals?" When we answered yes, he said, "I believe you, so I am not even going to make you take the written tests; however, you will need the vision test." After doing this, we suggested that we had better leave. In passing, we remarked that we were looking forward to seeing the autumn leaves. With this, he jumped to his feet to introduce us to a lieutenant, saying, "He knows all about the best places to go to view the leaves." The lieutenant gave us a cup of coffee and introduced us to the rest of the force. After forty-five more minutes discussing the beauty of Pennsylvania and the merits of hunting, Chuck said, "I really must go." The friendly lieutenant walked us to our car and encouraged us to come visit again. I had always been aware of our Texas hospitality; this encounter was to be only a beginning, a forerunner of Pennsylvania hospitality. Pittsburgh may be sooty, bleak, and smoggy, but her heart is as big as the three rivers she embraces.

Given my Achilles heel concerning the health of my daughters, I placed finding a capable pediatrician high on my priority list. An able doctor was recommended. His office was very close by. When I called to make an appointment (the schools required certain checkups), I was graciously told, "Sorry, we are not taking any new patients." With my intellect, I could understand the possible necessity for such a policy, but with my heart I felt cold, stark rejection (later on this doctor was to accept us as patients). Thus, when Heather and Laura hopped in to tell me they had each stepped on rusty nails, I was instructed to take them to the Passavant Hospital emergency room for tetanus shots.

This catalyst punctured my balloon, and out floated all the pent-up emotions, resentments, and frustrations. Would life ever, ever settle down for me? I was tired, tired, tired of this whole "shooting match" of events! Never had I seemed to work so hard and to accomplish so little. If only I had my friend, Ida Mae, to bail me out once a week! Not only could I not locate any capable help, I could not even start on the search. In Pittsburgh our budget would not include a maid.

Before the girls had hobbled in, a surly policeman had come to my door, informing me that Buffy, my shaggy dog, was loose. He warned me of the strict leash laws and said that the next time he found Buffy out he would fine me fifty dollars! With so many children going in and out of my front door, how could I ever hope to keep Buffy from the clutches of the law? And why did I pray for all of those children to be in this neighborhood, anyway?

My feeling of martyrdom had been accumulating for days. Chuck, of course, was nowhere around in this new emergency. He was off in the big city of Pittsburgh working in the Lord's vineyard. Daily he was in fellowship with many Christian men. I had not yet found a Bible study fellowship group for me, and I needed it desperately. I grabbed my car keys, growled at my two girls to "get in the car," and started off to locate the hospital.

The emergency room was a busy, crowded arena of life. After giving the necessary information to the secretary, I sat down to wait my turn. I was feeling so sorry for myself caught in the maelstrom of unimportant, tedious, bothersome happenings — inconveniences, flies upon my pane of orderly living. I was thinking only of my needs being met, most certainly not being "mindful of the needs of others." As I sat and waited and watched, I saw pain and suffering encased in bodies both young and old. I saw bleeding bodies, broken bodies, burned bodies, and suddenly I thought, "Lord, forgive me! I have no real problems, only a few pesky gnats flying across my window pane. I think I thank you for allowing me to come to this place today."

As I continued to wait, a man, a frantic father, rushed in with a bleeding child in his arms. The man was crying, "Oh, God, somebody help me." The child was quickly taken through the Do Not Enter doorway, and the man was left in the waiting room. He seemed consumed with love, fear, and compassion for his small son. He was so distraught over this little boy that he was unable to give the vital information to the hospital secretary. While one of his neighbors very calmly gave the necessary data, the man anxiously stopped a nurse and said, "Tell him that his daddy is waiting and that he loves him." Looking at the two people, the father and the neighbor, I thought, "What a contrast!" There is such a difference between a father's love and a neighbor's love, between that of a shepherd and a hired hand; both are caring, but to different degrees.

I walked over and tried to comfort the man. He told me that he had four sons and that each seemed to get into trouble, to get hurt. He had gone through this same agony before with each of the other boys. This was the baby. His heart was so stretched in caring for sons.

I thought, "Lord, if that man, that father who is still so cloaked in his raw humanity, can care so much for one of his little ones, then how much more must you in your perfect love care for me, and mine, and all of the others?" And I was reminded again that I had a Heavenly Father who was waiting — and who loved me.

As I left the hospital, I was thinking, "I must try to remember to trust you more with me and mine, to trust you with this whole risky business of life and living even in this strange, cold, new homeland." I must try to appreciate and cherish the "now" moment. Later I wrote:

We really *do* have only the "now." We possess nothing more. We have only this present moment to
laugh,
   love,
      listen,
         be true to,
            pray,
               sing,
                  reach out,
                     mend,
                        touch,

> forgive,
> move,
> be still,
> work,
> just "be."

Yesterday will be no more; those clouds have wafted into eternity; tomorrow, for me, may never come in this world; as quickly as that can a world change! Why do we, do I, always assume that my feet will forever be making footprints in the sands of this world? Why do I risk postponing important commitments, chance dismissing valuable ministries in assuming that I can always "produce" on the morrow? Not so. The present moment is the "now." This present moment is the most important moment in my walk through eternity; I can only deal with brokenness here; I can only reach out to the lonely now; I can only praise God in this corner of this hour. I can only forgive in this small segment of time. I may repent, repay, sing, or say the words that need to be tumbled forth only in this "now" moment. This is the only currency that has merit, that I can cash. The past is already a receipt, and the future is only a promissory note. How can I dare to waste what will never, ever come again? This present moment in God's story?

I shall *not* use up or squander my precious todays in yearnings for a past age that might have been, or in fearing for a tomorrow that may never come. God has only promised me grace sufficient for this one day. He gave the manna in the desert only to meet each day's need; the Israelites could not use yesterday's food or store up for the tomorrows. My God is a God of the "now." He meets me with power in the present, in the "now." Since he has never failed me, dare I not risk trusting him with all of my yesterdays and tomorrows? If I am continuing to walk with him in his story, he will most certainly continue to fill my heart and my hands with many things to do for him here in this "now" kingdom.

O God, I pray that I may always remember to polish this present, precious, "now" moment!

And for the rest of that one day — I remembered.

14

Marching to the Pittsburgh Drum

By the end of September, Chuck and my girls had eagerly accepted their adopted homeland. They were marching to the Pittsburgh drum, but I was singing "The Eyes of Texas." Chuck was traipsing around the streets of old Pittsburgh, trying to familiarize himself with his new "parish." He loved his work! Every morning he even seemed to enjoy walking across the long Sixth Street Bridge. Although that walk was often raw, cold, wet, and windy, he was so innoculated by the dynamic spirit of his adopted land that he seemed unaware of his own discomfort.

The Pittsburgh Experiment has a Sunday night radio show. Chuck enjoyed this new dimension to his ministry. Because of his engineering background and interest, Chuck asked the radio engineer to explain every detail of the equipment. The engineer enthusiastically responded, "You are the very first person who has come in here that has ever asked!"

Besides his Pittsburgh Experiment work, Chuck became actively involved in the Episcopal Diocese of Pittsburgh. The bishop appointed him to serve on the Board of Evangelism. Chuck was also on the list of supply preachers; so he was able to continue with his ecclesiastical and sacramental responsibilities as a priest which was very important to Chuck. Nearly every Sunday found him starting out through those twisting turning roads in search of his assigned church.

Occasionally the girls and I accompanied him, and we were intrigued by the antiquated church buildings hidden in the many small boroughs. Especially were the girls fascinated by the old churchyard cemeteries. Sometimes it was difficult to disengage them from reading the faded old tombstones. Chuck was working hard in his new vineyard and loving every minute of it!

There were not enough daylight hours for Heather and Laura to do all they dreamed of doing! They loved exploring the woods around our house and viewing the wildlife. There was always someone ringing the doorbell and questioning, "Can Heather and Laura come out to play?" There were two small "crises" for them, however. The first occurred the day of the University of Texas and Penn. State televised football game. The girls had eagerly decorated our house, our mailbox, our yard. Anything that could be reached had an orange and white banner flying from it. They had boasted to the entire neighborhood that Texas was Number One and would stop and stomp Penn. State. There was no sign of humility or compassion in their loud declarations! When the Longhorns emerged as victims instead of victors, the girls were left holding a sack of sawdust words and bruised egos. Wide-eyed, Heather and Laura gasped, "We can *never* face our friends again, *never!*" As the friends gathered out front with taunting shouts of, "Who's Number One?" the girls went slowly outside to face the crowd. Never again did they boast, "We are the greatest."

The second unexpected small happening was precipitated by our love for Mexican food. All of us missed our enchiladas, tacos, and tortillas. One day we were so desperate that we decided to try to make our own tortillas. We had brought with us massa flour and a small iron tortilla maker. With much trial, error, and failure, we finally produced fifteen tortillas, three for each of us. As much as Heather and Laura loved tortillas, they decided to make the supreme sacrifice by sharing their precious allotment with some of their friends. The girls had been boasting about the greatness of Mexican food. Taking a hot, buttered, salted tortilla in hand, they ran outside to share. Each friend who took a bite, spit it out in gagged disgust. This was almost worse than the insult to their Texas Longhorns!

For only a little while Beth Ann felt lonely and alone. She received a thoughtful note from John Knox.

> Our best wishes to you as you begin life in your new house, neighborhood, city and state. It will be strange if you — or at any rate some of you — don't feel "displaced" and homesick for a little while. But as you settle into your house and get acquainted with your neighbors, and Chuck with his job, this feeling will pass, I know. And don't ever forget, there are many hearts in Austin (not to speak of Houston and San Antonio) where you will always be "at home" wherever you may be in time and space.

Beth Ann's daily trips on the school bus plunged her into the reality of life and living. Mass meanness was a new experience for her, but since she was the "new girl," she faced certain school bus initiations. Either she was barred from sitting down, purposely tripped as she tried to walk down the aisle, or covered with "unbaptised" language. Daily the loud conversations overheard on the bus ranged from instructions on shoplifting to choices of ways to deal with unwanted pregnancies. Beth Ann chose to deal with the whole bit of the bus grievances by herself. It wasn't until the initiation rites had long ceased and she had become accepted that she shared the problems. In her steadfast, gentle fashion, she had worked through her own situation without worrying us. She, like her daddy, is usually one of those steady harbors in the midst of a storm.

Beth Ann became involved with a Wednesday night fellowship group which met in one of the large Presbyterian churches. She found a group which "sounded her sound," so she was "home free." And she found a special friend, a girl named

Kathy, who loved all of the things that Beth Ann loved. Since Beth Ann was very enthusiastic over her classes and teachers, she was soon singing again. Her prophecy of "doom" sounded while still in Texas had long since been forgotten!

As I watched my family blend into their new surroundings and adjust to new circumstances, I wondered why I was still so out of step. If only Chuck had come as rector of a parish! Then I would have a nest of people waiting to love me. I was not a part of his city ministry. This was a man's world. I could not even meet Chuck for lunch; he was always busy "doing his thing." My Christian friend, Olyva, lived forty miles away, so I did not get to see her very often. My neighbors were very friendly, but they were all so busy with their own concerns. And as far as being busy, I was constantly working trying to keep my salt-box in functioning order. How I missed Ida Mae! As I saw the stack of ironing mount, I kept wondering, "When is someone going to do that ironing?" I had not ironed in twenty years. Then cold reality breathed down my neck. No Rumpelstiltskin was going to appear to spin my straw into gold, my ironing into completion, my dust into rubies, or my tarnished silver into polished wonders. With the "somewhat" help of my three girls, I was going to have to be my own Rumpelstiltskin! At times I even worked hard in shoveling snow or breaking up ice. The "taken for granted" walk to collect the mail often took a pioneer's stamina just to brave the elements and win the victory of opening the icycle-clustered mailbox.

I even had garbage (they call it "rubbish") problems. I was told that I was limited to two garbage cans. They picked up only once a week, consequently I became very "trash" conscious. If someone gave me a gift, I was torn between two attitudes — one of joy and anticipation over receiving a present, the other of "Will this tissue paper and cardboard fit into my weekly allotment of trash?"

Grocery shopping required another adjustment. Back home, a young man was always at my elbow saying, "May I carry your groceries to the car?" I shall never forget my first shopping spree in Pittsburgh. My cart was spilling over with groceries and other necessary items. I stood patiently waiting for someone's offer to help. Finally I said, "Excuse me, where is the carry-out boy?"

The answer came loud and clear, "Lady, *you* are the carry-out boy. We have no such thing." Weekly, as I struggled to push the always wobbly cart to my car, often in the rain or snow, I would have to work on my attitude. As I stumbled forth shouting my resentments at the weather, the grocery store, my plight, I would make a willful effort to work on my attitude. I would try to say, "Now, Carolyn Huffman, think of the many people who would shout for joy over the privilege of having this much money to spend on groceries and would welcome the effort of pushing this wobbly old cart even in the snow and rain. 'Yes, Lord, that's right.' " And I was all right for that one shopping spree, though I would usually have to play a repeat performance the very next week. I remember hearing a speaker quote the psychologist, Victor Frankl, in saying, "Ultimate freedom is the freedom to choose your attitude." It was a constant struggle for me to choose rather than to absorb my attitude.

15

What Would I Say?

School had been in progress for only a few weeks when I read the article in the paper: "Paul, a sixteen-year-old, was killed Thursday while he was playing goalie during a game of soccer." Immediately, I felt such fierce compassion for the boy's mother! And I thought, "What would I say — what could I say to another mother who had just lost her son?" With these words ringing in my ears, I found pencil and paper.

Lord, how do I write to another mother who has just lost a son? How did you in all your transcendent glory and majesty withstand the loss of your son, Jesus? He knew compassion for all the unrighteous, thus all of us. How did you keep your world in orbit? It seems as if the universe surely would have fractured and been torn completely apart from the agony of that whole affair upon the cross. How he must have suffered; how you must have suffered for all mankind on that day.

What can I really say to another mother who has just lost her son? Should I tell her that I still remember the cold, frozen pellet pain in the pit of my stomach, the numbing of the senses? How well I still remember that even the grass had lost its green, and the sky had lost its blue; everything was void of flavor, color, and shape.

Should I tell her that the first year of having grief as an escort is like having someone inside your head spreading searing hot coals across the brain? That each first birthday, Easter, Mother's Day, Thanksgiving, Christmas, is anticipated with such horrendous, fierce despair that when the dreaded day finally arrives, so much energy has been used up in sheer dread that the actual day holds fewer dragons than had been imagined?

Have you ever walked along the shallows in the sand when, as if from nowhere, in swift surprise, you find yourself almost knocked down by a maverick wave? Shall I whisper to her that this is the same, precise feeling of walking along the shallow sands of grief, emotions thought to be completely under control, when with no prior warning, a tidal wave of sudden remembering, a calling up of the memories, knocks you flat? You find yourself drowning in your own agonizing grief, fighting for your very life's breath! With the passing of time, the tidal waves do diminish, and the storms do decrease; however, I know that the tidal waves in my sea of memories will never completely disappear as long as I live in this world, nor would I choose for them to do so.

And should I warn her of the devastating homesickness, or the desperate, indescribable longing to be with your dear one? That hurts the most. You shout, "Surely, it is time for this nightmare to be gone, to be over, to be banished, to be cast into utter darkness from whence it must have come! Surely it is time for me to return to the reality of life, of living, the place I walked before this nightmare commenced, before this dream enveloped me. But the nightmares continue and even seem to intensify. The mantle of heaviness becomes so stifling you feel certain that you will stumble and fall under its massive weight.

And what of morning's first conscious moment? Shall I hint at what that will become? On first awakening, there is the tiny, split second that you find yourself in confusion, knowing, perceiving that something is surely awry, not quite right; then the silent, scorching screamings inside your head begin to remind you of what has actually happened, to alert you to your new address, "Agonyville." You feel that you will remain in this place forever. The audible moan that escapes is summoned forth by the shock of the scepter of death lying there on your pillow waiting to greet you again, and again, and again — and again.

Should I tell her that grief so completely consumes you, so directs you that you find yourself functioning more like a robot than like a person, and responding to others as if they were no more than sticks walking around on a stage? You are certainly not a participant in this drama of living; you simply do not acknowledge these sticks at all, for they might try to penetrate the wall that you have so carefully constructed. You surely don't want anyone to slip behind this fort, for then wouldn't they see the open wounds and the broken fragments that once made up a heart? A heart that concludes that none other in history has ever suffered such painful ruptures of tissue!

Should I delete from my letter the part concerning the loss of memory? Perhaps this mother will experience it. I found in grief that I could so train and drill and condition my mind to repress the many unbearables of sorrow that I found myself also forgetting even the simple data of living.

In what I write to her, I must remind her that grief often points an accusing finger at God. You find yourself shaking a fist and even cursing him. For surely, this is his world, and his plan, and he is most certainly responsible!

And what of those who really try to help? I must assure her that there will be many. Shall I warn her of them? Of the ones who sincerely try to assuage the pain? Of the friends who will try to persuade you to open your tightly clenched fist? The fist that is holding on so desperately to the grubby, dried-up crust of self-pity, hurt, anger, resentment, pain, suffering, guilt, sorrow, indifference, and distrust.

Voices are saying, but you are not hearing, "Open up your hand, relax your fist, and allow the dried-up curd of all your sorrow to fall; open your heart to allow God's healing love to begin its work." (Beginnings, though small, are so important, are giant steps toward the road back; no, toward the road ahead!) Voices are saying, "Relinquish this loved one to his Father; turn him loose, release him! Don't you know that God in his perfect love loves this child even more than you love with your mother's heart?" God will not, even with all his power, force or pry open those numb, frozen fingers! You can spend a lifetime of starvation just clinging fast to the grubby crust while God's bountiful banquet of gifts and fruit stands as close as one small word of acquiescence, a yes to the living, flowing grace of God.

Voices, voices, so many voices . . .

Very carefully, I must relate to this other mother that I finally started to listen; that I began slowly to uncurl each finger, one at a time, until the fist was no more, but instead, a palm held up in praise!

Out of my experience of grief, I shall try to console this mother. But how can I adequately explain to her that, miracle of miracles, the world slowly, very slowly began to change, to come back into focus? The grass became green again, the sky became blue, and the hazy, black sticks started acquiring faces! Happiness began seeping in, then overflowing beneath the door of my cell, my self-locked cell, my own private prison of pain and self-pity, my private room of darker than dark.

I must emphasize that slowly, very slowly, I began to allow God's healing touch to balm and mend and patch the shattered pieces that once made up a heart; this self same heart was thus enlarged to hold not only me and mine as before, but to contain some of God's other broken people. I even started loving him more, and more, and more, and still more.

Lord, I pray that this mother can experience the same paradox that I have experienced, that of seeing my life's greatest sorrow transformed into my life's greatest joy, the reality of knowing and loving you.

Will she believe that I can now say, perhaps often only whisper, "Thank you, Lord, for taking this savage suffering of mine and transforming it into creative suffering." And, also say, "Thank you for loving me and allowing your own son to die upon the cross for me and for others like me."

I do praise you, Lord, for the knowledge of the reality that life here, in truth, is just for a season; that some day, I shall surely see this son of mine, this child of yours, again. I shall see him face to face and know and be known by him!

Thank you for the pure, passionate joy I have discovered in trying to walk with you in your story. And although I still stumble and fall often, although there are still precipices ahead, I know, believe, and trust that you will remain faithful in sustaining me and that nothing can ever separate me from your love.

Truly, now, how do I speak to another mother who has just lost a son? I cannot, for only you, Lord, can reach down that far into the depths of the dark night of the soul! I can and will pray that she will listen.

16

What Must a Person Do to Find God?

In October the leaves changed. For centuries poets have described this metamorphosis, and artists have hinted at the beauty of nature's handiwork. But, like my encounter with God, I had to see and experience autumn myself to appreciate its true wonder. The hills of Pennsylvania were on fire with color! I might have been persuaded almost to believe that the legendary Rumpelstiltskin really had appeared and transformed the trees into rubies and gold! But why did the beauty span such a brief period of time? In two weeks the myriad fairyland had been both created and abandoned. Now the trees, bare and forlorn, were left standing with only a memory of their coronation finery.

October found the girls busy and happy although they were adjusting to "Pittsburgese." For example, one didn't "spend the night," as back home; she "slept over." One didn't request a rubberband; one asked for a "gumband." One didn't say "you all"; she said "you guys." The girls discontinued giving the University of Texas "hook-'em-horns" victory sign when they discovered it to be an obscene gesture when rendered in Pennsylvania!

Chuck was becoming more and more immersed in his new ministry. Now he was enthusiastic about the approaching Oglebay Conference. Yearly the Pittsburgh Experiment had a weekend couples' conference in Oglebay Park, Wheeling, West

Virginia. It was to be held the first week in November, and Chuck was excited.

I was still treading water. With my intellect and with my body, I lived in my salt-box in Pittsburgh, Pennsylvania. With my heart, I still claimed residence in Texas! Nearly every night found me physically exhausted for I was working so hard. One evening I was especially weary; during the day I had relished the thought of an early bath and a prompt slide between the sheets of sleep. As I prepared for bed, I could hear happy voices downstairs where Chuck and the girls were watching television. Reaching to turn out the lights, I stumbled across some thoughts which demanded my attention! The words that confronted me were, "What must a person do to reach the top, to find God?" and the answer came, "He must be willing to start." Though my body was bone weary, my "head" became adrenaline alive! I decided to consider the question more fully.

What must a person do to reach the top, to find God?
He must be willing to start.

What if he loses the way?
The path is marked very clearly; if he gets lost,
he can find his way again, if he is only willing
to open his eyes and see.

Is the way to the top, to God, a dangerous journey?
Yes, a very dangerous journey; why, people have been
known to lose their very lives!

Why then would anyone ever start?
Because never to start at all means certain death,
death to true life, to the abundant life; people have
found new lives in seeking the summit.

Is it cold?
Yes, often it gets very cold, so cold that one wonders
if the inner spark, the fire, has gone out completely,
but it never does; only let the spark get close to the
Source of fire again, and the flame is soon rekindled.

Does it ever get too hot?
Oh, yes, sometimes the heat of God's Holy Spirit
searing away the dross and purifying the soul can
become very uncomfortable, even painful, but this
does not last forever.

May I take someone along to guide me? I get lost
so easily. There are many, many guides, and they
come in all guises. He himself is never very far
away; his helpers are legion; sorrow, pain, joy,
suffering, success, failure, aloneness, and love all
are able guides in directing climbers up the mountain.

Must I climb this climb, walk the path, start out
on this journey myself, or may I send someone in my
stead, pay someone else to represent me, and tell me
of the great adventure along the way? I am faint
hearted, and get weary, you know. No, this is a
journey that you must make yourself; don't worry
about being slow; he has a different path for each
traveler, but you must go yourself to behold his true
glory; oh, others can try to tell you of the reality,
to speak of the wonder, but it is never quite the
same.

May I turn back and quit if I so desire?
Oh, yes, but once taste this adventure, and you
will never be the same again!

What do I have to lose?
Only your life.

What do I have to gain?
Only your Life!

Then let's begin!

Weeks later I was working at my desk. Close by was a copy
of "What must a person do . . ." Heather came into the room,
picked up the copy, and began reading. There was a silence,
and then she said, "Mother, did you write this poem?" When I
answered yes, she continued, "I wish I knew God."

"Why, Heather," I replied, "you *do* know God."

Her answer came very softly, "Not the way you talk about it in that poem." I realized that this was no idle conversation. She continued, "I want to get to know him better."

"Heather, there is a long word called *commitment;* it means telling God that you think he can run your life better than you are running it yourself. You ask him to come into your life and be the Lord of your life; you commit; *you turn over,* you give your life to him, and ask him to be in charge."

Thoughtfully, she said, "I want to do that. Will you help me with the words?" So with my encouragement, Heather said, "Lord, I give you permission to come into my life, and be Lord of my life; thank you, God, Amen." About thirty minutes later, she ran downstairs and whispered in Chuck's ear, "Daddy, I read mother's poem, and I just committed my life to Jesus Christ." In Sunday school class the following Sunday, she shared with the whole group, "I read my mother's poem, and I made a commitment. I asked God to run my life."

A friend had written that she was very discouraged and depressed about certain crisis situtations in her life. As an afterthought in answering her letter, I slipped inside a copy of "What must a person do to reach the top, to find God." Several weeks later she replied:

Carolyn, I just had to add another note about your writing. When I finished reading it, I just broke down and cried and cried! It was after that that I decided to write you more about my quandry. Several hours later, my daughter came home from school; I read the dialogue to her. "Sure," she said, "did she *really* write that?" Then I read it to my psychiatrist yesterday morning. He was quiet for a minute, then took out his handkerchief and wiped his eyes. He asked for a copy of it to be read to his family at the Thanksgiving table. I had it Xeroxed and took a copy to him. Since I've had ten copies made, I'll send you back your original. I intend to keep mine where I can see it every time I get a cup of coffee — inside the cabinet door in the kitchen. Thank you again for sharing it with me and others.

Remembering the limp, tired state of my body and soul the night I wrote that piece, I was staggered at the results! It was incredible that God, even a God of the universe, could so successfully work through such imperfect instruments!

Oh, God:
I am *so* little, so puny.

How can almighty you pause to do business with
failing, faltering, sinful me?
Are you sure that I am your needed instrument? This
is ludicrous. Haven't you noticed the broken, blunt,
snarled, twisted ends? The tangled pieces, the
rusted parts?

Haven't you seen the faulty, counterfeit, unreliable
instrument that I really am?
Don't you think that you should really reconsider
your choice, look more carefully on this great earth
of yours?
Surely, surely, there must be countless others who
are much more cleaned up, polished, refined, tempered,
beautiful, and far more reliable than I.

It has been said that you perceive all things.
Have you so forgotten the many times that I failed
you? Refused to speak up for you? Denied you?
Disliked you? Disobeyed you? Forgot you? Neglected
you?
Surely, Lord, there are many servants who have allowed
you to reign on the throne of their life much more
than I. My humanity, my self always seems to get
in the way, and I understand Paul when he says:

"It seems to be a fact of life that when I want to do what is right, I inevitably do what is wrong. I love to do God's will so far as my new nature is concerned, but there is something else deep within me, in my lower nature, that is at war with my mind and wins the fight and makes me a slave to the sin that is still within me. In my mind I want to be God's willing servant but instead I find myself still enslaved to sin. So you see how it is: my new life tells me to do right, but the old nature that is still inside me loves

to sin. Oh, what a terrible predicament I'm in! Who will free me
from my slavery to this deadly lower nature? Thank God! It has
been done by Jesus Christ our Lord! He has set me free" (Rom.
7:21-25, Living Bible).

It is such a mystery! I bow my knee to the mystery.

17

Getting Back
in the Wheelbarrow

It was almost November. Anticipating the Oglebay Conference, Chuck was getting more and more enthusiastic. I was getting excited too. For just a little while, perhaps, I could participate in his ministry. His new assignment had presented me a role change. In seminary and at St. David's Church, I had enjoyed being involved with Chuck in his work. In Pittsburgh, this was not the case. Daily Chuck would make his thirty-minute drive, walk across the old Sixth Street Bridge, and become immersed in his city ministry. Before I could put faces to the names he mentioned; in Pittsburgh I rarely ever saw the faces that went with the names. But occasionally, Chuck described some of his experiences, and I could vicariously participate in his ministry. Often he would rush in and say, "Let me tell you what happened in the group today."

Of all the groups, I believe the Employment Anonymous Group touched Chuck the deepest. It had been started by another Pittsburgh Experiment member who had taken Sam Shoemaker seriously when he said, "Get changed, get together, get going." This man felt a burden for the unemployed men in the city, and there were many. After doing some research, he discovered a pattern to their malady, a crippling syndrome. After a period of unemployment, a man felt himself to be such a failure as husband, father, friend, provider, that not only was he unemployed, he often became unemployable. Appearing for a job interview, he often aired the attitude of "You don't want to hire me, do you?"

So this Pittsburgh Experiment Christian caught hold of a dream. Why not form a group of men who could uphold, strengthen, and spiritually support a man while he was living in the frightening land of unemployment? Sometimes, on the wave of the backwash, an actual job offer arose, but this was not the group's purpose. Every Tuesday a gallery of men, including a Ph.D. chemist and a few disadvantaged alcoholics currently residing under the Sixth Street Bridge, gathered for lunch at the YMCA. Many just slipped in for a free meal. In general Chuck felt it was primarily a "soup kitchen" operation.

Then one day Chuck had a guest, Ed, the Presbyterian minister whom he had met at the Congressional Prayer Breakfast. Chuck was anxious to show Ed the mending and outreach he had seen manifested within the group. In the middle of a serious conversation, two participants began a verbal battle, loudly slinging drunken curses at each other across the room. "I'm gonna stick this fork in your eye!" shouted one man. Someone finally succeeded in silencing them, and the meeting continued. Chuck was embarrassed for his friend to see such a botched-up meeting; obviously, there would be no healing and mending that day. The occurrence seemed to parody the basic purpose, magnifying the men's main interest — the warm meal they were about to receive. They appeared impervious to any deeper or higher message.

The closing circle of prayer began. When it reached Snuffy, the first disrupter, he was silent, and then he reached way down into his bundle of memories and softly began to pray, "Now I lay me down to sleep, I pray the Lord my soul to keep. If I should die before I wake, I pray the Lord my soul to take. Amen." When it came his turn, Snuffy's counterpart started to speak but couldn't — he just sat and cried. But that was all right too, for by this time there was not a dry eye among God's motley crew.

Another day a young man from India came into the Y for lunch; seeing he was alone, one of the Pittsburgh Experiment members asked him to join their group. He assented. During conversation over lunch he shared the fact that he was a computer scientist from India and unmarried. Weekly he kept returning to the group. One day he said, "You know I don't know anything about your Jesus Christ. I came from a background of Hinduism, but God has never been real to me. My life is empty. I go to work, read, and play chess — that's it. I have heard you men talking about a thirty-day prayer experiment. Can you participate from a position of nonbelief? Tell me about it." The men explained the thirty-day program that Sam Shoemaker had started years ago. For thirty days, you ask God to come into your life and meet you at the point of your greatest need — just that. You don't tell God how to solve your problem; you just trust him to meet you in the midst of it. The Indian agreed to try the experiment. I don't know exactly what happened. I do know that later he came by the Pittsburgh Experiment office and said, with new joy in his face, "Hey, I want to commit my life to Jesus Christ!"

I could get excited as Chuck related these stories, but I missed the first-hand contacts, so I was eagerly awaiting the Oglebay Couples' Conference which I would share with Chuck. One evening, a week before Oglebay, we were having dinner with Maggie and Paul. I turned to Paul and said, "Tell me everything about the conference. Start at the beginning and go through the whole schedule."

Paul started, "On Friday afternoon, the staff will arrive. Everyone else will start arriving around 6:30; we will have dinner, then afterwards we will have our first meeting. I will speak first, then Chuck will speak, and then — *you will speak!*" Paul got no farther; in fact, he had already gone way too far! I was staggered by his announcement. I could see a portent of another rickety wheelbarrow ride! I wanted to participate in Chuck's ministry but not this fully! Again, I was faced with the choice of "fish or cut bait," "put your money where your mouth is," believe that God really is trustworthy and faithful in his promises. I agreed to speak, but Maggie's delicious cooking had suddenly lost its luster.

After reading some things that I had written, Keith Miller once said, "Carolyn, you should write a book." Others had echoed Keith's admonition, and from time to time the words surfaced into my consciousness. I persistently pushed the idea beneath the waves, but like bright red beach balls, the words kept popping up when I least expected. On the Monday morning before Oglebay, they assualted me again. Faced with a trumpeting injunction, I did something that I can't recall doing before or since — I made a deal with God. "All right, Lord, if you really want me to write a book, then give me some more affirmation. If I don't get it, I'll know I'm not to write a book, and I shall consider the subject closed." With this entreaty, I concluded the matter had been attended to, and I turned to what I thought were more important things.

What was I going to say at Oglebay? I was scared. I told Laura that I had to speak in front of many people and that I was frightened. She asked, "What are you going to speak about?"

"Oh, I will just tell what God has done in my life."

At this, Laura enthusiastically said, "Oh, mama, that will be easy! God has been so good to you."

Oglebay Friday arrived. I loaded my "wheelbarrow" into the car and headed for the beautiful country around Wheeling, West Virginia. After we arrived, I helped in registration. Many people were repeaters, anticipating new insights and new wholeness from the conference. Others were first-timers; for them, anxiousness often blended with anticipation. I sympathized. I was anxious too. The familiar pattern had begun —

pains in my stomach, diarrhea, and a total disinterest in food. At dinner I counted the peas on my plate and hid my meat behind the mashed potatoes. With one part of my brain, I tried to carry on an intelligent conversation, and with the other part, I mentally rehearsed my talk.

With about four hundred people present, the meeting began. Paul Everett, an excellent, buoyant speaker, reminded me of a ringmaster at the circus. He was so glad that everyone had come and so excited about his "show of shows." Paul told several funny stories, and the audience responded with gales of laughter. Then he introduced the next "act," Chuck. Chuck too was in a vibrant mood. He also told some jokes, and the laughter was again loud in response. Then Chuck spoke of the series of events that led him to Pittsburgh and sat down. I heard the "ringmaster" announce the next event — an aerialist act, Carolyn Huffman was to attempt to cross the high wire in an old rickety wheelbarrow.

I approached the microphone and told the audience that I did not know any jokes but that I would not tell them even if I knew some, for this was no joking matter to me. I was frightened (Chuck later told me that the tail end of my skirt shook the entire time). Then with my voice very steady, my thoughts as clear as a bell jar, no notes, I spoke about the God who wanted to do business with me and with them. I told of walking in his story and of always finding him faithful and then read "What must a person do to reach the top, to find God." I sat down, greatly relieved that my act was over. I had made it across to the other end! I planned to enjoy the rest of the conference. I was hungry too. Where was the cotton candy?

On Saturday night I sat beside Chuck. It was a comforting feeling to be in the safe, warm womb of the audience. Pastor Harley Swiggum, a Lutheran minister from Madison, Wisconsin, was to be the keynote speaker. He was the author of the Bethel Bible Series, an adult Bible study that was meeting with great success all over the country. I was anxious to hear

what Harley Swiggum had to say. He approached the microphone, paused, and then started speaking. "Before I give my
address tonight, there is something I feel I must say. It is my
business always to be on the look-out for good communicators;
last night I saw a very frightened young woman get up on this
stage and speak. Carolyn Huffman, you have been given the
gift of communication. You must speak more, but, Carolyn
Huffman, you must write a book!"

My friends tell me that Harley then gave an outstanding
address. I didn't hear a word, for I was playing hopscotch across
searing thoughts. My cheeks were aflame, and I felt as if
everyone in the auditorium was shining a flashlight on me!
This was only Saturday. I remembered my words so carelessly
flung out to God on Monday morning. "Lord, if *you* want *me* to
write a book, you will have to give me more affirmation." I
wouldn't have dared to set the standard so high as to say,
"Lord, if you want me to write a book, just have a tall, slender
man get up on the stage and make the announcement before
four hundred people!" After the meeting, I raced up to Harley,
grabbed him by the arm, and gasped: *"Why* did you do that to
me?"

He answered, "Carolyn, I hated to embarrass you in front of
all of those people. I've never done this before, but once
someone did it to me and got me started on my writing career.
It was no idle whim. I thought about it all day. I was under
conviction. I *had* to do what I did tonight!"

Oglebay was over. Many agreed that it had been an
excellent conference. We headed back to Pittsburgh. I tried to
settle down and sleep, but I kept hearing the penetrating
words, "Carolyn Huffman, *you must write a book.*" Well, I
wouldn't think about that now; I would put that in my box
labeled "for future consideration."

18

Leave of Absence

Outside it was November, and it was November in my soul as well. As I waited for Heather to finish her piano lesson, I looked out the car window over hills of ice and snow. I was homesick and thinking of the coming holiday season. Back home the family Thanksgiving turkey would be eaten, and the Christmas tree would be trimmed, and we would not be there as part of the festivities. If only the distance weren't so far! If only I could visit that warmth for just twenty-four hours! I would give hugs to so many! As I viewed the cold, stark landscape, I thought, "You know, the Bible is right; we really *do* have seasons of the soul! And I am living in my winter season right now."

At times my heart feels as cold as the glistening snow now piled up outside my window; and, sometimes, a wintry blast within the core of my soul seems surely to have blown the heat of God's Holy Spirit far, far away. The fire seems to be almost gone, nearly extinguished during this winter season. In fact, some days I am not even aware that there is one solitary ember of God's Holy Spirit left glowing anywhere within my being; no apparent vestige remains. The interior of my soul resembles a bleak, cold, wintry day with no flame upon the hearth, and no God upon the heart. So many Christians in the past have written of the "dark night of the soul." I would add, "the cold dark night of the soul." No trace of God anywhere upon my cold horizon; I feel that the glass is all frosted over causing my vision to become impaired during this winter season of my being.

I wrote to John Knox concerning my loneliness and my feelings of displacement. He wrote several letters of comfort, one of which included the following paragraph:

> We do hope that by this time things look brighter for all of you. They are bound to soon. You must be sure of that. And your life in a strange, frustrating environment will become life among many new friends and opportunities; and who can say not? Perhaps richer than life was here in this familiar place. God can turn even our frustrations, failures, and despairs into creative resources — as Paul reminds us in Romans 8:28: "We know that in everything God works for good with those who love him, who are called according to his purpose."

And in another letter, he said:

> I sympathize when in connection with speaking of the fact that you are having "growing" experience, you say that you sometimes ask each other whether "so much growing is really necessary." If we were together, we would probably laugh a bit over such a question, but it is really a serious one, and I think it must be answered affirmatively (or at any rate should be answered as if the adjective were "good" or "desirable" or "worthy," instead of "necessary"). Of course, such an answer presupposes that one is not "growing" away from what is one's true self, separating oneself from one's roots — which, needless to say, would not really be "growth" at all (but death) and of which neither of you is in the slightest danger — but are not true "learning" and true "growth" always good?

Later John also wrote:

> I recognize how ... troublesome it is as you face a stay of indefinite length away from Texas. I knew before you left that you would feel a special difficulty in adjusting to being so far from "home" (as so many thousands and hundreds of thousands in our culture have to do) because you are the particular person you are and because of the multitude of close, intimate personal relationships you have here in Austin and in this region. But though greater in *degree* in your case, perhaps, the same difficulty of

adjustment is felt by *so many* from time to time that maybe, *just on this account,* you may become more patient of it. Lois and I were much moved by your speaking of the "effort" you have to make daily to be "joyous." Robert Louis Stevenson uses somewhere the phrase "the great task of happiness" indicating that, for him at least, happiness was both an *obligation* and not always an easy one to fulfill. It is so, I suppose, for all of us, wherever we are and in whatever circumstances. It is bound to be so for you, even here in Austin at any rate occasionally. I felt, and I think all of your friends did, that your joyousness was God's gift, as all true joyousness must be; but is it not a fact of the spiritual life that God's gifts, free as they are, presuppose on our part so deep and active a desire that it cannot but mean also an effort? It is man's "extremity" which gives God his "opportunity." But this "extremity" lies at the end of our trying our utmost, and then, and only then, throwing ourselves on his mercy and grace, which is always waiting to bless us. All of this you know better than I. I have looked up the poem of Stevenson's of which I recalled a line. It may be good to quote it:

> If I have faltered more or less
> In my great task of happiness,
> If I have moved along my race
> And shown no shining morning face,
> If beams from happy human eyes
> Have moved me not; if morning skies
> Books, and my food, and summer rain
> Knocked on my sullen heart in vain;
> Lord, thy most pointed pleasure take
> And stab my spirit broad awake.

The poem as a whole only partly applies to you and your need, but it does point to the only healer, "The Celestial Surgeon" (the title of the poem).

I should be surprised if eventually you and Chuck and family were not back in Texas, if not in Austin, and I imagine that you and Chuck think and occasionally talk of such an eventuality. But it may be a long time off. And meantime perhaps, without forgetting it entirely you had better let it recede into the background of your thoughts. It is probably true that it is good for Chuck to have experiences as a pastor and priest that he could not have had here, and good for both of you to live for a while, possibly for a long while, in a very different environment than Texas provides. Such new experiences and needs for adjustment as they are having may well be good for the children too. And if Romans 8:28 is true — as we all know it to be — the time will come when you will think with gratitude and joy of your stay in Pittsburgh. All of this you know, and I apologize for saying it, but we all know, too, that in this respect or connection as in so many others, we simply are unable to realize with our *emotions* the truths we know with our minds, especially sometimes.

At the time I was reading John's letters, they offered me solace, but sooner or later I would begin to "move among my race and show no shining morning face." I read my Bible, grasping for truths there. And, remembering how meaningful Paul Tournier's book, *A Place for You,* had been, I began to reread it.

So there is always in life a place to leave and a new place to find, and in between a zone of hesitation and uncertainty tinged with more or less intense anxiety. If the division in the mind is violent, it can take on the dimension of a disease, in the form of an anxiety neurosis. But this is only a more dramatic paroxysm of a tension that is inescapably present in all of us, and which shows itself at every critical turning-point in our lives. There is a past security to be lost before we find a new security. No security lasts, however solid, just or precious. For it is a law of evolution and tomorrow will not be the same as yesterday, and that there results from the difference the anxiety of today, since each moment is a middle zone between the past and the future. . . . The rhythm of life goes on, carrying us along with it. It does not stop to wait for us. I thought of the trapeze artists, swinging on their trapezes high up under the dome of the circus tent. They must let go of one trapeze just at the right moment, to hover for a moment in the void before catching hold of the other trapeze. As you watch, you identify yourself with them, and experience the anxiety of the middle of the way, when they have to let go of their first support and have not yet seized the second.

. . . But we must not carry the analogy too far: the trapeze artists are engaged only in a game; whereas life is a serious matter, in which we are concerned with successful living rather than random leaping. When God gives us riches and then takes them away, it is so that he can give us more valuable riches still and bring us to true life through both of these movements.[1]

To John Knox's letters, I could affirm loudly, "You are right"; to Paul Tournier's book, I could say, "I believe what you have written." To the Bible I could say, "I do believe, help my unbelief." But, I was still hanging over that frightening middle zone, afraid to release my trapeze bar of home in order to grasp the dangling Pittsburgh bar.

One bleak day in November I returned home from my weekly struggle with the grocery cart. Pittsburgh was gray, cold, smoggy, raw, strange, alien. What was I really doing way up here anyway? I was tired of choosing my attitude! I would just absorb Pittsburgh's grayness! I was tired of working at the great task of happiness. It was warm inside my salt-box. My bright red carpeting was certainly more cheerful than outside my window! I felt safe inside; so I made my decision.

Lord, you remember I have spoken up for you many times in the past. I have tried to walk with you in your story, even crawled inside that rickety old wheelbarrow! It is cold out there, and unfamiliar out there, and I get lost so easily. I have decided that I am going to become a "bump on a log." When we get back home, we will pick up our story where we left off. I will continue to believe in you, but I will stop doing business with you.

Now, that took care of that!

19

Bloom
Where You Are Planted

Thanksgiving had passed, and Christmas was upon me. I went through the motions of celebration, for my joy had slithered down some rabbit hole. Each day was a heavy burden to be carried. Grumbling and unloving, I met every morning with a complaining, critical attitude. Everything the girls did seemed to be wrong. Chuck could do nothing right. Even the dogs fell under my wrath. They were always in the way! I was miserable and homesick. I felt a lostness, a crushing of spirit. I carried around a bucket of complaints and could find nowhere to dump them. They just seemed to accumulate, one on top of the other. Though I was certainly aware of my state of unhappiness, I was not yet ready to allow the cure.

New Year's Day arrived. Stretched out ahead, 1972 taunted: "What will you do with me, Carolyn? Just how will you juggle all my days to fit into your scheme of things? Will you color me black? Will you limp through each month, dragging your bleak soul behind you?"

No! I would not! I did not want to color this new year gray, much less black. Something must be done about my attitude. I wrote to John Knox: "St. Davids' Bookstore has a poster, a bright pink and red flower with the words *Bloom Where You Are Planted* written upon it. Will you please have them send it to me? I am still very homesick and am not blooming at all This might help."

I hoped the poster would arrive soon, for I could not stand sharing my skin with my grouchy self much longer.

It was Saturday, January 15, and Pittsburgh was draped in a somber, smoggy, gray cloud, a cloak of bleakness flung over her shoulders. Not even my red carpet helped. I heard Chuck shout, "Carolyn, the mail has come, and John Knox has sent you something!"

I knew exactly what it must be — the poster. And, as I looked outside at the heavy mist, I also knew that today I certainly did not choose to bloom where I was planted. Instead, I chose to absorb my attitude — grayness. So I hollered, "Just put it down on the hall table. I know what it is. I'll open it later." I continued to choose to hold close my dismal day.

Monday morning brought the usual scurry for lunch money, misplaced books, lost mittens, and just plain grouchy sleepy natures. Finally, the children had walked to the school bus, and Chuck had driven away to the city. I was left all alone with myself. I poured a second cup of coffee and picked up the package from John Knox. It needed to be opened. If I wanted to discard my chrysalis of embracing depression, then I had better take some action. I tore off the brown paper and unrolled the poster. How bright was the pink and red flower. I read the message: Bloom Where You Are Planted. The poster didn't say, Bloom Only When You Are in Texas or Bloom When You Feel Like It, or Bloom When the Sun's Out. No, it said, Bloom Where You Are Planted. I tacked up the poster on my den door and then just sat and looked at it. What in the world was the matter with me anyway? *Why* did I lack blossoms? *Why* had my growth been so retarded? What was *really* wrong with my "plant"?

Here I am in a foreign land, on different soil, midst a strange people; strange, chiefly because their culture and customs differ from mine. Strange also because the faces that belong to the bodies walking around are unknown, unfamiliar to me. Where are the precious features of the dear ones I know so well and love so deeply? I am close enough to those to know the heartbeat and sense the pulse of their very lives. It was so very safe, warm, and comfortable back home in the nest; back home where I knew and was known, where I loved and was loved, where I ventured and felt safe in the trying; home seems so far away.

Is life then to be a continuous embarking, a wrenching away from the safe, the known into the very vulnerable circle of the unknown and the incalculable? Will we become stagnant if we choose to confine our outreach, our daring, our adventures, our risking to the safe, secure, controlled circles of life? If we choose to remain in the eddys that we can adequately handle, safely navigate, with only an occasional call to a God, a comforter, a savior, will we be quenching the Spirit?

The large colorful poster with the bright pink and red flower reads: Bloom Where You Are Planted. Since I have been in this foreign land, on this different soil, midst these unfamiliar people, I have seen very few blossoms on my vine, very little blooming at all; I have wondered about this. How can there be continual blooms without any healthy roots? Just how long can a plant survive without roots caressing some soil? How long can a soul be healthy, produce fresh buds without the roots being put down, extended into the soil of God's people? Can I ever expect to bloom if I refuse any rooting of my being in this strange soil that surrounds me, that holds me so close?

Oh, I know that one can never transplant completely without leaving a trace, a vestige of the roots in the original plant bed; these pieces will remain there always; roots, however, must be set down again in deep, rich, growing soil of love and relationships, or the plant suffers, seems to wither, and becomes a pale image of its original vital self. Sometimes, it suffers so from the lack of sufficient water, food, air, and proper soil that one would wonder if the plant has become diseased or impaired.

So, this day, I shall remove my plant from "safe" storage where it has been so carefully hidden away awaiting the return journey to home and happiness; I shall gently unball the burlap and attempt to begin to allow the fragile root fingers to start reaching down and out into this most unknown land; I shall try not to control or set limits on just how shallow or how deeply these roots should burrow, or how long this plant should remain in this place; I shall even try to refrain from digging and bothering the roots to see if they are truly taking hold, becoming secure.

I shall expect new buds and full blooms to appear on these tender, vulnerable shoots, but not because of any uniqueness of my plant, of any special quality of my soil, or of any rare obedience of my heart. I shall anticipate these new growths only because of my availability to God's unfathomable ability; only because of my allowing his ray to fall and penetrate the foliage; he has the love and the ability, the power, to care for, to prune, and then, miraculously, to transform tired, ailing, wilted plants into vital instruments of glory for him.

Two days later, I very unemotionally said, "Lord, once again, I give you permission to use me as your instrument; I *do* want to do business with you; I *do* want to walk with you in your story." After past experiences with prayer, I should have known to start fastening my safety belt and preparing for a roller coaster ride of thrills! I was about to be back in the wheelbarrow business!

Two days later the phone rang. It was Beverly, a Presbyterian minister's wife, calling. She said, "Carolyn, in about six weeks our church wants to schedule a weekend retreat for our women. Will you be the retreat leader?"

"But I have *never* before been a retreat leader!"

Her reply was, "That's all right; we have prayed about this, and you are our choice. We think that you can do the job."

I told her I would call back to give her my answer. I panicked just thinking about it. How could I ever hope to hold forth for an entire weekend? How could I possibly accept? It was out of the question! And then, I remembered — only two days ago, I had said, "Lord, I *do* give you permission to use me again as your instrument; I *do* want to walk with you in your story." It was the old wheelbarrow bit all over again. Either I believed in God's promises and would act upon them, or I didn't. It was that simple. I had trusted God before to be true to his word, to be faithful. Now I had no choice. I had to be true to my promise. I called Beverly and told her I would be their retreat leader. Though I might know very little about leading retreats, God knew everything!

Two days after the call concerning the retreat, I received another phone call: "Will you please be the World Day of Prayer speaker?"

I groaned, "What is the subject?"

The woman's answer was, "I do not have that information yet, but I will have it tomorrow. Let's leave it this way — if you can identify with the subject, then you speak; if not, then we will ask someone else." I agreed. I also hoped that the subject would be something like "Sex Life among the Great Killer Whales" or "When Is the Second Coming Really Going to Come?" She called back the next day. The subject: "Through Sorrow, Can a Christian Still Know Joy?" I said, "That's my story. I'll talk." And, again, though the body was shaky, and recalling the gray days painful, the voice was calm. God was there, and he was faithful.

Two days after the World Day of Prayer phone call, Chuck phoned from the office. An engineer from J and L Research Lab who had been at Oglebay had just called him. Once a week at J and L around one hundred engineers gathered on their lunch hour to hear a Christian speaker. They were inviting me to speak! What in the world could I say to one hundred engineers! But, remembering my offer to walk with God in his story, I whispered yes. Though I might not know what to say to scientists and engineers, he did know.

The J and L Research Lab was some distance from the city, so Chuck offered to drive me there. We took Bridge A instead of Bridge B and consequently arrived at the lab five minutes late. My worried host was waiting on the steps. He pinned an entry badge on us and said, "Hurry!" We ran down a long corridor and stopped in front of a door. When our host threw it open, I saw a large group of men sitting there just staring at me. Their faces said, "Well, girlie, you are late — and what can you have to say that would interest us, anyway?" And I was frantically thinking, as I caught my breath, "What in the world do I have to say to you, anyway?" I had certainly prayed that God would use me; I just hoped he hadn't taken a wrong bridge too! As my host was introducing me, the calming thought came as if God were saying, "Carolyn, you really *do* have something to say. These men are like all my people; they have the same hurts, the same pain, the same fears, the same broken dreams, the same need for me. Tell them about me."

"That's right, Lord." So I took a deep breath and began: "God really doesn't ask us to understand him; he only asks us to be obedient and to walk with him in his story, and he will give us our lines, one at a time." Afterward, many of them came up and affirmed what I had said. Several suggested that I write a book, but that idea was still filed away back home.

And so Pittsburgh's grayness began to diminish. I began to feel the old joyousness again. I often sensed God's touch on my shoulder, and I had located a Christian fellowship group. This was the balance I so desperately needed. I also had a new friend, Sister Mary Therese, a Roman Catholic nun who brought much warmth to my soul. Chuck continued to take me with him as he led retreats, and he had me telling about this faithful God who wants to do business with his people.

It was February 26. So much had happened since the January morning when I had agreed to "come out of retirement." Reflecting over the past events, I was almost breathless.

Lord, last month I gave you permission to use me again as your instrument, as imperfect and as impaired as that instrument might be; I said that I was willing, for a little while anyway, once again to "walk with you in your story."

How you can *so* take these meager crumbs, these minuscule offerings, these fragments, these bits and pieces of almost nothingness, and use them for your glory is incredible! How you can so take that small grain of commitment, that particle of faith, that wee bit of obedience to your will, and transform it into something of power, of substance, of value, of joy, of love, of service in helping you to further your kingdom is unfathomable!

Only God could create a pattern, a design that could so transform a tiny acorn into a giant, sturdy oak, a dried-up wispy-looking flower seed into a fragrant blossom of beauty. Who else could program a perfect rose to emerge from a craggy, ugly, thorny, wooded stalk? Only you could call forth a bounding babe from a fragile fetus. And only you could take my small, scattered pebbles of commitment and faith, so carelessly thrown out on to the water, and produce ripples of love and meaning, your love and your meaning for other lives to share and to touch.

What if I had not said the words, "Lord, I give you permission to use me once again as your instrument; I do want to continue to walk with you in your story, to share your great adventure." Would you, patiently, have allowed me to sit there forever caressing my curd of self-pity and fondling my statue of self-importance? But, you *knew*; you perceived that once I had really tasted life, the reality of the abundant life shared with you, that my soul could be nourished by none other; that once having danced with kings, having sung praises with other Christian pilgrims, having experienced the indescribable joy of being your person, having dined in the kingdom, your kingdom, having drunk from the cup, that I could no longer choose just to exist, barely exist in that other land of paupers; my appetite, once whetted by your reality, can be satisfied now by no other food.

So, once again, help me to allow this earthen vessel, this old crockery jar, to be broken for you, so that your treasure, your spirit, your love, your joy may shine forth for all to see.

20

Jesus Christ Superstar

On March 10, Chuck's and my wedding anniversary, Chuck was out of town, and I was lonesome. I invited my friend and neighbor, Laurie, over for a cup of coffee. Later, realizing the time, she said, "I must rush home and set up sixty-six chairs. Herb and I are having the Sabbath meeting at our house tonight. The rabbi is going to discuss *Jesus Christ Superstar* and the Jesus Freaks." I loved the music of *Superstar* and responded enthusiastically to her statement. Laurie said, "Carolyn, would you like to visit our meeting tonight? You are welcome." I told her that I would love to come; so it was all set.

That night when I arrived, the religious service was over. The side table was laden with good food, and everyone was eating and visiting. A friend introduced me to the rabbi, a young seminarian who was to graduate in a few months. My friend said, "I would like for you to meet Carolyn Huffman; she lives right down the street."

With this the rabbi said, "Wait a minute — don't tell me — her husband has a little church somewhere!" I explained that Chuck did not have a little church somewhere, but he was a Christian minister.

The visiting was over, and the rabbi continued the meeting. I sat on the front row beside Laurie. Before starting the record, the rabbi gave his opinion of the Jesus Freak movement. Many of the people present had expressed concern because some of their teenagers had been confronted by the Jesus Freaks. The rabbi tried to put balm on their fears. He assured them that they had nothing to worry about. He considered the Jesus Freaks another fad in a long line of American fads. They could dismiss their worry. Then he started talking about the record, *Jesus Christ Superstar.* I was fascinated by the dialogue which ensued, thinking what a privilege it was to be included. I wished for Chuck. Many of their teenagers, along with their Christian peers, had been exposed to this record. Some of them had even come home and asked their parents, "Is it all right for us to *talk* about Jesus just as long as we don't *believe* in him?" (Isn't that what we Christians do all the time?) Many questions were brought to the meeting, and most of them were asked by men. Just before playing *Superstar,* the rabbi said, "Now, listen carefully, and tell me if you think this record is anti-Semitic — against the Jewish people."

We all listened intently. The record was familiar to me, for our family loved the music and played it often. But this time I listened through different ears; I tried to hear it as a Jew would. When the music finished, many hands went up. Not one person felt it was anti-Semitic. Then, one man said, "What I would like to know is what do the *Christians* think about *Superstar?* I would think that some of them would not like it." There was a pregnant silence. I was the only Christian in the room. Laurie kept nudging me with her elbow, "Get up, Carolyn. Get up and speak." So I shot up a quick prayer of help, stood, and anxiously began.

"Well — you are right. Many Christians do not like *Jesus Christ Superstar* because it stops short of the resurrection. In no way can it ever be considered the full Christian story; nevertheless, I feel *Superstar* probably gives us a very realistic picture of the week before the crucifixion — the climate, the chaos, and the confusion that must have surrounded the event.

Surely the question on everybody's mind and lips was, Who is this man Jesus?

"Now, you remember the Jesus story one way, and you have come up with one answer. I remember the story about Jesus another way, and I have come up with another answer. But we are all faced with a serious question: Just who is Jesus of Galilee? The question demands an answer!

"As for the Jesus Freaks, I guess I see that differently too. I believe that when a person accepts Jesus as his Lord and Savior then the Holy Spirit comes to dwell, to live within, and he truly is a different person and can never quite be the same again. But here again I bring one experience to the story, and you bring another."

With this last statement, the rabbi jumped to his feet and said, "You are right, and that is not my experience." There were several questions from the group concerning Christianity, and I was grateful for my years of participating in small groups, for the times that I had to try, however feebly, to articulate my faith, or listen to someone else try to articulate his faith. None of my answers had to be brainstormed off the top of my head.

After the meeting, several men came up and talked with me. One remarked, "As a young man I was in a Russian synagogue; *never ever* would the word *Jesus* have been uttered; it would have been unheard of to discuss him the way we were doing tonight; times have changed."

An older man said, "As a child, I was taught that there were absolutely no discrepancies in Holy Scripture; now I see that there are many minor discrepancies."

I responded, "But that hasn't done anything to shake your faith in God, has it?"

He replied enthusiastically, "Not a thing!"

They were so kind to me that evening. I was invited to return and was given a Jewish Prayer Book. Later under the section for silent prayer, I read:

O, Lord, I shut out the din and fret and littleness of things that I may feel myself alone with Thee in the silence. As a child yields itself to loving arms, I yield myself to Thee, asking for nothing, complaining about nothing. What if my labor is hard, what if my lot is humble, what if my dreams turn into futile tears, if only there is the peace of Thy nearness in my heart. There comes to me in the stillness, despite the terror and tumult of life, a trust in a goodness that nourishes the roots of the grass blade, that glows in the flaming star, and attains fulfillment in the soul of man. How healing and strengthening is this communion with Thee, O God. If only I could always abide in it. But I must go forth again to the struggle for daily bread, to the restlessness of desire and the fear of pain, to the disillusionment of dreams that never come true. Let me not go forth alone, O God. Abide Thou deep in the solitude of my heart, that I may trust in Thee and be unafraid in the face of the inscrutable years, and see that everything happens for the best. Amen.[1]

It was late. Clutching my new prayer book, I said goodnight and walked home. I was exhilarated from my experience. When I reached home, Chuck was waiting. "Where have you been?" he asked.

"Happy Anniversary," I said, and then, "I have just been having a marvelous time — witnessing before the 'Sanhedrin!' "

I never dreamed my wheelbarrow would roll through a Jewish Sabbath meeting.

21

One Small Blue Trunk

I spent most of April trying to encourage and entice spring. In Texas I had never been aware of spring's actual arrival. One day, in passing, I would just realize that sometime, without my conscious knowledge, spring had swept into town and dressed up all of the trees in tones of green. Her early appearance was taken for granted. In Pittsburgh, April had come, but it had not yet encountered spring. During the month, I examined many a bough looking for that first bud, that first sprig of life, but to no avail.

I kept my salt-box in working order and spoke for different church groups. Spring had not come to Pittsburgh, but it had come to me! Walking in God's story again brought new life to my soul.

One day I decided to organize the garage and happened to open a small blue trunk. Unknown to me, Chuck had transferred Carl's things from a cardboard box to this small blue trunk. Opening the box and glimpsing the contents, I gasped out loud! Once again, just the sight of the favorite toys and precious drawings took my breath away. With tears streaming down my face, I rushed upstairs to settle my soul and calm my upheaving spirit.

How *can* a heart remember so long? From *whence* do the threads come? The threads that are tugged suddenly, vibrantly, and so very violently? And from whence springs the memory? A memory almost as fresh as the day the mourning first began? It is almost as if a portion of the soul had been securely wrapped and buried in the sand when, powerfully, a wave breaks across the shore unwrapping and exposing the soul, and revealing every single, screaming raw fiber of its being.

Thirteen years, Lord — thirteen years is a long time for a small lad to be away, a long time of missing, and hurting, and crying, and yearning, and thinking, and remembering him. I am lonesome for his touch — I am homesick for him.

How strange, and really quite unexplainable, that the chance opening of one faded blue trunk disclosing a small boy's treasured mementoes and childishly drawn pictures could so cause such a sudden fracture of the membranes of the heart, and such a quickening of the breath, and such a coldness in the stomach; that an old rag doll, small wooden wagon, favorite straw hat, Steiff toy monkey, and a broken toy boat that has long, long ago lost its luster could cause tears to race to the surface and erupt like an exploding volcano. And why did these tears still have such a raw, fresh, flavor?

And, another question — why do I even choose to cherish and hoard this small trunk with these precious possessions when I can scarcely even bear to open the lid? When I know, and truly believe, that my son surely has no more need of these treasures, or even need of me, when he has Thee? That my son is not really as close to me in these faded old mementoes as he is truly near to me in the spirit; in the kingdom of God, we are so close. I don't know *how* this is so; I only know *that* it is so! I know this as surely as I know that I can reach out and touch my shaggy dog on the head or smell the fragrance from the red flower in the bowl. I know and fully believe that some day I will see Carl face to face. And I believe that he has been growing from strength to strength in his realm, just as I must try to grow in mine.

How impossible it truly is to try to glean, understand, estimate, or even attempt to measure thy great and perfect love, O Lord. For, if my human love can still so passionately flow forth, spill out after the span of all of these years from only a chance glimpse of an old rag doll, and a crazy straw hat, then what must be the capacity of love poured forth from a loving heavenly Father?

To be a mother who loves a son so is surely a witness to the reality of love. To have a heavenly father who loves me, us, the world even more is surely a gift that can never be comprehended — only accepted.

And, Lord, I thank thee again, for the privilege of having those brief years with that dear son of mine, of thine; despite the ruptures, scars, snags, and splinters still left within my heart, I would not for one moment sacrifice the joy of having him to escape the pain of losing him. It just hurts so to remember; I praise thee for being the great physician who knows not only how to mend hearts, and erase tears, but also how to transform abrasive sand into priceless pearls of reality.

22

Lowing All the Way

During the first week in May, spring finally paid Pittsburgh a visit. I wanted to shout to everyone I met, "Do you see the trees? Have you touched the leaves? Have you looked at the hills? Have you thrilled to the tulips and crocuses? Are you really aware of life throbbing all around you and screaming out loud?" I saw, and touched, and loved that very first spring in Pittsburgh in a way that I had never before responded to spring.

Besides spring, other important reasons made that particular May special. I will never forget May 16. It was 5:00 in the afternoon when the phone rang. Effie introduced herself and then said she was the program chairman for the Methodist church. She continued, "We are having our district meeting tomorrow morning; sixty-five churches are involved. Our speaker has just called from Baltimore to say she is ill and cannot come. Will you be our speaker?"

My head and heart and stomach turned cartwheels! Sixty-five churches! I felt as if this time the Lord really was carrying things a little bit too far. but he had always been faithful in the past, so why should I renege on him now? I took a deep breath and said, "I'll be your speaker. What is your subject?" When she replied, "Bloom Where You Are Planted," I could not believe it! My whole body felt like one big enormous funny bone that had just been bumped!

With no finesse at all, I screamed out at the poor woman, "Just who told you about *me* and "Bloom Where You Are Planted"?

She replied, "Why, no one. Several months ago someone heard you speak at a World Day of Prayer service on 'sorrow.' When I heard about this, I just mentally filed your name away. Funny, but when the speaker from Baltimore called to tell me she could not come, yours is the first name that popped into my head."

I was still stunned, but I had myself a little more under control. "Listen, I don't know what God has in store for us tomorrow, but I am your speaker. I wrote a meditation on that very thing in January! I'll be there."

The next morning I was calmly expectant. I could hardly wait to see God in action! Before, whenever I talked, I always suffered loss of appetite, queasy stomach, and much apprehension. Today I suffered no disorder. In fact, I felt just great! I knew that, for this one time for sure, I really was walking in his story! I was really doing business with the God of the universe — the one who decreed the boundaries of the seas and who commanded all the mornings to appear. No one ever could have persuaded me that this episode was coincidental.

When I arrived at the church, I was handed a program. The front was covered with bright yellow daisies and red, red petunias. At the very bottom, beneath the flowers, was written: Bloom Where You Are Planted. Inside was the Baltimore speaker's name; instead they should have had: Speaker — Yahweh, using the old wobbly, cracked, crockery jar, Carolyn Huffman!

That day I told the story about my "leave of absence" from the God business. Then I showed them the poster and read my meditation. They seemed amazed at the unfolding of events. Later one of the young women came up and said, "My husband has been in the ministry for a number of years. In the past whenever God 'called me,' I just dismissed him and turned him over to my 'answering service'; I have never been able to believe in Divine guidance, but I cannot dismiss what happened here today. I have made a new commitment of my life to the Lord, Jesus Christ."

Another woman commented, "The thing that disturbed me is your saying that there is a difference between just believing in God and in doing business with him. I must go home and think more about that."

Another brilliant young woman had been trying to come to the faith through a scientific formula. She was first trying to discern the nature of God before giving him her allegiance. She said that I had given her much to think about.

That day was one of those "ah-ha" moments in my life. God seemed so close and so real. What could ever top this experience?

Later, I heard from Sue Kinney who had heard me speak. Several months afterward, her seventeen-year-old daughter, Shawn, was killed in an automobile accident. She wrote:

> One day, about a month after Shawn's accident, I stood by her grave crying, thinking in spite of all God had done for me, that I simply could not go on. I cried out to God to help me, and I heard a voice within say, "Bloom where you are planted." Could I do this? I came home and tried to put my thoughts down on paper.

> Bloom where you are planted . . .
> But I am planted in the Valley of Grief,
> Planted there by one cruel, senseless accident of life.
> The Valley is deep.
> Its walls seem insurmountable.
> Yet at the top a Ray of Light.
> I must grow tall to reach that Heavenly Beam.
> Each day the Ray grows stronger.
> I struggle as a tree reaching forth my branches
> To meet the all sustaining Light.
> Clouds gather to obscure my Holy Vision.
> I wilt. My roots are shallow, but the Heavenly Dew pours forth
> My soul refreshed, the clouds part and once again I see
> that Radiant Glow.

My buds struggle to burst forth from their leafy womb.
Oh, Lord, let me bloom here in this Valley.
Let me bring forth the glorious fruit as you intended,
And let me reach that Holy Light which is my Life's goal.

On Thursday evening of the week following my eleventh-hour talk, the telephone rang. It was Carol, a Christian friend, calling with a specific request. "Carolyn, our Presbyterian minister, Paul, and his wife, Lee, are going to Scotland. They had planned to leave on Monday; however, Paul has just received a call from his travel agent telling him that it is imperative for him to leave this Saturday. We want to know — will you fill the pulpit at the 11:00 service on Sunday?"

I really groaned over that question. I told her that I could not give her an answer yet, that I would just have to think about it, and pray about it, and silently to myself I thought, and try my best to get out of it. I told her I would call her back. I guess I had placed an imaginary sacrosanct circle around the 11:00 worship service — around the pulpit. It was sobering even to consider doing such a thing. No, I really didn't think I could handle this assignment. God was just pushing the two of us a little far this time! It wasn't fair! I felt as if he was really putting me on the spot! Perhaps I could think of a legal, valid way to weasel out! I ran downstairs and questioned Chuck, "Don't you think that some of those Presbyterians might resent the idea of having a *woman* in the pulpit?"

Chuck said, "Carolyn, I would like to help you out, but the Presbyterian church has been ordaining women for years — sorry."

I went back upstairs to be alone with my thoughts. I could not find one valid reason for refusing! But what did I really know about Presbyterians? What could I say to them? And then I remembered — the Lord knows all about Presbyterians too, and this really was his deal, not mine. I would just have to trust him to see me through once again. I called and agreed to speak.

That Sunday morning I awakened with the usual queasy symptoms. It was the "speaker's malaise" again. Chuck and the girls had been invited to attend church with me and to stay later for lunch. This was not at my suggestion! I had not planned to invite them, would have preferred that they stay at home or go to their own little church somewhere, but they did have to eat, so I told them that they might as well come along. All four were in high spirits that morning. They were in a teasing, hilarious mood, joking about the possibility of my wearing Chuck's collar. They even threatened to tape my talk and reminded me I would probably have to process down the church aisle. They were all having a rolicking good time!

After checking what each girl was planning to wear, I informed them all that I was leaving. They could just come when they came, but I wanted to get there early. (I never understood before when Chuck used to tell me that very same thing! Oh, walking in those same moccasins unravels many a mystery!) I also wanted to be in the car alone so I could have a long talk with God — remind him that I was counting on him to be there!

I was right. There really is something about the 11:00 hour on Sunday morning that is sacrosanct. It was scary too. I had already processed down the aisle, and we had finished with the first hymn, but there was no sign of my jolly family. Shortly before I was to speak, I saw them sheepishly slip into the back row. And what a conglomeration of garments one of the girls had selected to wear! That was certainly *not* the outfit she was planning when I left home! And look at the shoes! They were just terrible.

Oh, me, I bet the prophets of old didn't have to put up with such problems! And then he was introducing me, and the Lord and I were "on." I began: "God doesn't ask us to understand him; he only asks us to be obedient, to walk with him in his story, and he will give us our lines, one at a time."

The service was over, and I was standing by the door. One little teenage girl took my hand and whispered, "I know what you are talking about; two weeks ago I gave my life to Jesus Christ." Others were also very gracious. Before speaking, I have always tried to remember to say, "Hey, Lord, if anything good comes from this talk today, let me remember it was *you* who touched me on the shoulder, and give you the credit, please."

I often have to work hard at reminding myself just who it was that had really written the script, who was really responsible for any success that might follow. My pride sometimes tends to roam like a lion, knocking down many of my Christian fences. I can easily get lulled into a counterfeit pocket of "puffed-up-ness." Someone can say to me, "You were so great," and sometimes I begin to believe him until something happens to jostle me and remind me that it is God who is great. He is the one who touched me on the shoulder, and the only thing I did was to have the courage to stand up in the first place. I remember that once in the Old Testament God spoke even through a jackass! And for a little while, my head is screwed on right again, but I can predict with unequivocal accuracy that pride will return.

In the many months to follow, I continued to say, "Use me, Lord, as your instrument; I *do* want to walk with you in your story," and he continued to do business with me. One rainy day I was on my way to speak at the First Presbyterian Church in downtown Pittsburgh. Since I had driven into the city with Chuck that morning, I arrived downtown two hours early. I looked at the magnificent church where I was to speak. It was *so* enormous looking, *so* overpowering! As I sat in the small room waiting for the two hours to disappear, I suddenly became very frightened. On the intellectual level, I kept telling myself, "Carolyn Huffman, for over a year now, you have been riding high in your wheelbarrow, and God has never once let you down. He has been *faithful, faithful – faithful!* Why do you think he will forget you today?" Mentally I could say, "That's right — I believe that!" But at the soul and stomach level, I continued to be anxious and panicky. I never use notes when I speak. What would happen if I rushed out to grab a passing thought and grabbed a handful of air instead? What if this time he wanted me to learn *humility?* I know he never gives promises of success, only asks for obedience, and tells us that we can trust him to be in the midst of it. Well, there was only one thing to do! As in the past, when my thoughts went crashing and bumping about, I grabbed my pencil, prayed *"Help me,"* and began to write:

Lord, here I go again stepping out in faith for you — scared. You have promised to go ahead and make the crooked way straight. Have you remembered this time? Can I claim your promise? Can I count on you? May I assume and expect you once again to meet me there? And guide me to say thoughts that are higher than my thoughts, in a way that is superior to my way? That you will put that special lilt in my voice, and joy in my face, and wisdom in my words that sing of you, and reflect your love and your kingdom? Will you surprise me again at the calmness of my voice in contrast to the screaming anxiousness of my heart? I claim your promise that you will give your wisdom to the simple — I am your simple. That your strength is made manifest in my weakness — I am your weak. And that your love can be shed abroad by your spirit through your instruments — I am your instrument, sometimes, a willing instrument, sometimes unwilling, sometimes obedient, sometimes disobedient — sometimes aware, sometimes unaware. Lord, in this "now" moment be with me as I step out for you. I step out — I trust.

And he was there!

The psalmist had really discovered a truth for himself when he declared, "Make me walk along the right paths for I know how delightful they really are . . . turn me away from wanting any other plan but yours . . . reassure me that your promises are for me, for I trust and revere them."

Now, on my better days, I agree with him; but there is another story in the Bible that seems to point to much of my performance. It deals with the old Ark of the Covenant which the Hebrew people believed to represent the presence of God. The Philistines had captured the Ark from the Hebrews. Now they wish they had never seen it. Idols have fallen, and a plague of boils has descended. The people are weeping and dying and blaming it all on the presence of the Ark. They want to get rid of it, but no one knows just how to get it back to the Hebrews. The priests and the diviners give them a plan: Build a new cart, fill it with gifts, and hitch the cart to two cows who have just had calves, cows that have never before been yoked. Shut the calves away from the cows, and place the Ark in the cart. If the cows leave their calves and return the Ark to the Hebrews, then they will know that it was God who brought this terrible plague upon them.

The people followed the instructions, and sure enough, the cows took the Ark back to the Hebrew people. But there is one little sentence tagged on the end of the story — the cows are reported to have been "lowing as they went."

Through so much of my walk in his story, I have been loudly lowing. I bellowed my way into his kingdom, the seminary, my first wheelbarrow ride, Pittsburgh, and other episodes too numerous to mention. Reflecting on certain chunks of my life, I can often say, "So, that's why God wanted me to go there." And sometimes, I can even say, "I am glad that my life-cart went through that prickly path or clattered down that hidden trail." Sometimes it is difficult even to remember why I set up such a loud, unseemly lowing in the first place.

It has been my experience that whenever I try to walk in God's story, he often adds dimension and color. Several years ago I dreamt that it was college reunion time. Chuck and I were together in a large room filled with people. A young woman came up to me and said, "I understand that you are married to an Episcopal priest. Is that right?"

I answered, "Yes, that's right."

She continued, "And I understand that you turned your life over to Jesus Christ, is *that* right?"

Again, I said yes. She hesitated and then asked, "Has it made any difference?"

In my dream I answered, "Let me put it this way — it's as if all my life I had a great big coloring book and a little stubby pencil. Then one day — someone walked in and gave me a brand new box of Crayolas!"

23

Happy Birthday

The morning we received the disturbing letter was a bleak Saturday. Chuck's mother had written to tell us that a very good friend of ours had just died. Not only did our friendship go back many years (we were all in college together), but Milton had been important to us in other ways. I always knew that if I needed him, Milton could be trusted to be there with the necessary answer. And now Milton was dead! *I could not believe it!* My brain refused to absorb such painful knowledge! I walked around completely covered by the mantle of the reality of Milton's death. He was so young! He had so much that he still wanted to do! It just wasn't fair!

A friend just died today. After a brief illness, he really died. He stopped smiling and talking and walking and running, and keeping promises, and loving, and laughing, and — living. He really died.

Strange to think that when the tulips are in bloom, he will not be here on earth to see them; that when the wind blows, he will not be here to feel its caress on his face; that when the sun shines forth, he will not be here to feel the warmth of the rays, and when it rains, he will not be aware of the moisture in the drops; he will not be standing on this soil to perceive whether the sky is a robins-egg blue, or black with the promise of night and all her mysterious stars.

And, what of his wife — he cannot ever again say, with Browning, "Grow old along with me, the best is yet to be." And what of his son

— he will miss being here with him as he grows from lad to a possible dad himself. Oh, how poignantly sad, how aborted life so often seems to be.

In my stunned thinking, in sorrow over my friend's death, I glean that I am really in grief for two today — for my friend and for me. "Not so," I want to say. Surely, I cry only for the death of a friend! In reality, however, inside the thinking maze inside my head, I hear the silent voices screaming, "It could be me, it could be me!" I could be the one missing the scent of the spring flowers, the caress of the wind, the precious touch of a child, the fleshnearness of a mate. "It could be me!" For isn't this to be my fate too? Surely, this earth's plan of life to death is irreversible. Some day the voice will come for me, and say, "Tonight, this very night, your soul is required of thee." And, what of me, am I building up treasures for myself here on earth, or treasures in heaven? Am I "being about my Father's business"? Or am I much more interested and involved in my own business? Do I acquiesce to the injunction to "go out into the world and tell them about Me?" Am I even familiar enough with the words to tell anybody anything about him? And, if so, would I be willing?

O Life, in your best moments, you are so very wonderful that the thought of whispering good-bye becomes 'untouchable.' O World, when you are all dressed up in your party clothes, beauty personified, you are supreme! Royalty! Why don't I "polish the moment" more often? It seems a tragedy that the script calls for us all to die, to leave this earthly realm. For, "God made the world, and it was good," so good!

Often, the joy, O God, of walking through this life in *your* story with you as guide is indescribable; just knowing your presence here, now, in this earthly kingdom is an awesome reality! Being in fellowship with other Christians brings forth truth to the promise of "life more abundantly." And loving my loved ones brings forth a special kind of joy.

In the past, all of your promises that I have claimed have been honored by you. You have been steadfast and trustworthy in every area of my life. You have never failed me, have never been too busy to hear me, or too transcendent to be immanent. Is it just not conceivable also that you have my death sojourn very lovingly taken care of too? Can I believe the words, "Eye hath not seen, nor ear heard, neither have entered into the heart of man, the things which God hath prepared for them that love him"? And, can I say along with George MacDonald, "If we knew what God knows about death, we would clap our hands"?

O God, I am so grateful that I have asked you to be in control of my life, to be my authority, my Lord; I am so relieved that the decision is not mine to choose the time to write "death," "finish" to this earthly walk; for, in my humanity, in my unknowing foolishness, I might choose never to choose! I might stay forever the blurry visioned caterpillar, eyes always on earthly things, and never sluff off this limited familiar body and accept wings to fly to the stars — and beyond! I might choose to remain a brown bulb, so fearful of being placed into the dark ground that I would lose forever the chance of becoming a golden daffodil dancing in the sun! Or, worse still, I might never have chosen to accept thee and life eternal, and would have then missed the court of the Lord of Lords, and the King of Kings.

O, friend of mine, dear Christian friend, what unbelievable things are you now viewing in God's heavenly kingdom? What angel choirs do you hear? What indescribable colors are you seeing? What old friends and loved ones are you greeting? What new lessons are you learning? To what royal crowns are you bowing? What goals are being set forth for you to accomplish? Have you seen Peter, Andrew, John, James, or any of the other saints? What of St. Paul? And, most of all, have you seen Jesus? Have you seen the annointed one, our Lord and our Savior? You will — oh, you will! We shall miss you here, but "praise the Lord," we shall meet again in that blessed realm of all the faithful!

For, death is truly a door to more instead of less,
  a plus instead of a minus,
    an increase instead of a decrease,
      a gift instead of a travesty,
        a filling instead of an emptying,
          an eternal instead of a finite,
            a *birthday* instead of a wake!

So, Happy Birthday, Milton.

         . . . and, *Happy Birthday, Carl!*

NOTES

Chapter 3
1. C. S. Lewis, *A Grief Observed* (Greenwich, Conn.: Seabury Press, 1963), p. 43.

Chapter 4
1. Helen Smith Shoemaker, *I Stand by the Door* (Waco, Texas: Word Books, 1967), p. xi.

Chapter 12
1. George MacDonald, "Obedience," *Christ and the Fine Arts,* ed. Cynthia Pearl Maus (New York: Harper & Bros.), p. 759.
2. Ibid.

Chapter 18
1. Paul Tournier, *A Place for You* (New York: Harper & Row, 1968), p. 162.

Chapter 20
1. *The Union Prayerbook for Jewish Worship, Part I* (Cincinnati: The Central Conference of American Rabbis, 1945), p. 336.